A LIVING HISTORY UNIT PUBLICATION

In Sickness and in Health

A history of Leicester's health and ill-health 1900 - 1950

by Clive Harrison

Acknowledgements

Many people have contributed directly and indirectly to this book through oral and written memories, photographs and illustrations, advice and enlightenment on aspects of health and health provision, comments and advice on initial drafts and making available facilities or other research material. I thank them for their help and patience.

Mrs G. Ayres (Leicester and County Convalescent Homes Society), Mrs J. Bass, Ms M. Cawthorne, Mrs J. Crowther, Mrs D. Greaves, Mr R. Gurr, Mr. L. Gutteridge, Mr Peter Jones, Mr and Mrs B. Jelley, Mrs E. Lilleyman, Mr T. Mattock, Mr K. Pearce, Dr D. Parkes-Bowen, Mr Norman Pilgrim, Mr R. Priestley, Mrs A. Robottom, Miss P. Russell, Miss F. Stoneley, Mrs L. Watts, Dr J. Welshman.

Staff at the Leicestershire Record Office.

The Editor of the Leicester Mercury, Mrs Shirley Aucott, and the Leicester Royal Infirmary History Museum for loan of photographs and permission to use them in this book.

The Editor of the Times Newspaper for permission to use an extract from an article (© Dr Thomas Stuttaford/ Times Newspapers Limited, 1998).

My wife, Olive, for painstakingly editing and correcting earlier drafts.

I acknowledge the role of Cynthia Brown, formerly of the Living History Unit, now in the Leicester Museums Service, who *'encouraged'* me to undertake this project in the first place and Angela Cutting, Living History Officer, who continued Cynthia's work ensuring the completion of the entire project. Both were gentle but persuasive!

Published by Leicester City Council
Leicester City Libraries
Living History Unit

Designed by Creativity Works

ISBN 1 901156 80 X

Contents

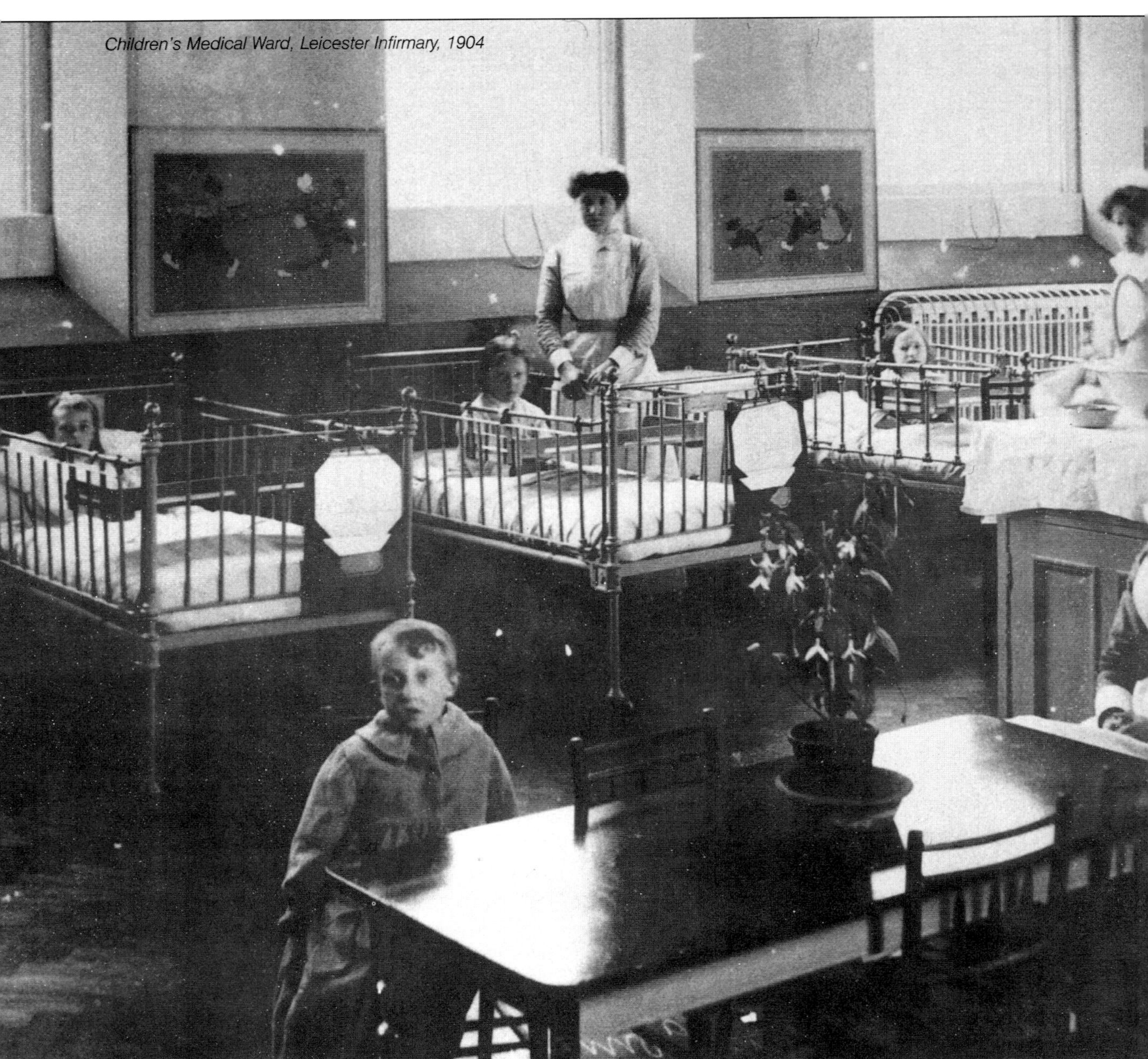

Children's Medical Ward, Leicester Infirmary, 1904

Introduction

What are your early memories of illness? What were the common ailments which you, your family, relatives and friends suffered from? Which ones brought death? Are they still around? Why have some ailments disappeared or are very rare? Are there any today which were not around in your earlier years or which were hardly known then? The answers to these questions will depend upon your age.

If you are over fifty or so, you are likely to remember: measles, diphtheria, whooping cough, scarlet fever and German measles which you had as a child. TB was definitely around as was polio and meningitis. People talked about someone dying of heart disease and, in hushed tones, of cancer! If you are over eighty, you might remember the flu epidemic of 1918-19 and possibly the tail-end of smallpox or at least have memories of these from your parents. Most of you in this older age group have memories of a new baby dying not long after birth and even a mother in childbirth. These are part of your living history!

If you are under forty or so you are definitely aware of heart disease and cancer and possibly have memories of TB. To these add meningitis, Aids, M.S., M.E., Alzheimer's and others - these are part of today but were almost unknown by the older generation, though that does not mean that they did not exist then. The ailments such as measles, whooping cough etc. mentioned earlier are not part of your living history.

We can next ask some further questions, the answers will again vary according to your age. Where were you born? Were you born in Bond Street Maternity Hospital, Westcotes Maternity, the City General or at home?

What happened if you were ill? Were you packed off to bed if you had one of the childhood diseases and were only mum and dad allowed in your room in case your brothers and sisters caught your germs? Were you excluded from school? Probably the doctor came to the house, not so common today! He knew you and your family very well. What did he prescribe? - not very much, no antibiotics, possibly a new thing called 'M & B' tablets and later penicillin. Did you have a mixture from the chemist or one made up by mum or grandma?

Which hospital did you go to? The Leicester Royal Infirmary, the City General, Groby Road Isolation Hospital, the Faire Hospital or the Fielding Johnson Hospital if you could afford it?

Did you go to a convalescent home? Roecliffe Manor, Swithland Manor or further afield to Overstrand Hall near Cromer, or Mablethorpe Convalescent Home?

How was this all paid for? The doctor, the chemist, the hospital and even the midwife had to be paid. Did your parents subscribe to one of the Friendly Societies or the Leicester Saturday

Hospital Fund, or the Leicester Public Medical Service?

If you were old and infirm and could not look after yourself, and your family could not help, there was the *'dreaded'* Hillcrest Hospital. If you were young and orphaned or your parents could not cope, you might have been sent to the Countesthorpe Cottage Homes.

There were various welfare and school clinics around the town, where nurses weighed you, dispensed dried milk, took out tonsils, cut out your verruca, pulled out a tooth, looked for nits and gave you spectacles. These will all be memories for older people.

For younger ones it is very different. There has always been a National Health Service with access to a range of services, originally free but now you pay something towards them.

Some of the hospitals still exist - the Leicester Royal Infirmary, the Leicester General, the new Glenfield General, they are all rather large, sprawling, somewhat impersonal places. Groby Road, Bond Street Maternity Hospital, Westcotes Maternity Hospital and Hillcrest Hospital have all gone.

Usually you go to the doctor, rather than he/she coming to you. It is likely to be a group practice and you see a different doctor every time you go, instead of one doctor who looks after you all your life. The average consultation time is three minutes.

You take your prescription to the chemist and most likely get a modern drug. Most of the old fashioned remedies have gone although patent ones such as Venos and Beechams are still around along with some new ones.

You are sent to the hospital for X-rays, a scan and many other tests and then the surgeons do wonderful things. You do not stay in hospital very long and you go home to get better.

Things have changed very dramatically!

This book looks at the various aspects of health, disease and health provision in Leicester during the first half of the 20th century. This period was chosen because it covers most of the dramatic changes in our health. The early years of the century were marked by legacies from the Victorian era - epidemics of often fatal diseases, infant and maternal deaths, poor health, limited cures, the Poor Law, poor housing and poor diet.

The end of the period is marked by the introduction of the National Health Service that promised to give all people free health and welfare care paid out of taxes. In between was a transition period marked by the eradication of many of the 'older' diseases and the emergence of 'new' ones, modest advances in medical practice, child and maternity care, the end of the old Poor Law, improvements in housing and the beginning of the Welfare State.

The book draws where possible upon the memories of people who are all now quite old. There are written accounts by individuals and reports of the Medical Officers, the Poor Law/ Public Assistance Boards, voluntary organisations and by newspapers.

It is a social rather than a medical history. The emphasis is upon the human and social history of health and disease as it affected the lives and attitudes of people.

Clive Harrison, December 1998

Part One

The Changing Pattern of Disease and Illness

There have always been constant shifts and changes in the pattern and incidence of disease over time. We can look at this process in two ways - by age-groups and by chronological periods of time.

Dr Charles Killick Millard, Medical Officer of Health (seated centre) and his staff, c.1927

Age-group

The main ailments which are relevant to the period covered in this book can be divided into four age-groups in terms of their incidence:

A Infants under 12 months: Summer diarrhoea, convulsions, atrophy and debility, lung diseases. Also included: premature deaths, still-born, miscarriages, ophthalmic neonatorium.
To these we would add many of those in B

B Childhood: Whooping cough, measles, German measles (rubella), scarlet fever, diphtheria, smallpox, chickenpox, mumps, scabies.

C Adolescence and early adulthood: tuberculosis (phthisis), rheumatic fever, smallpox, venereal diseases, maternal mortality, scabies.

D Mid/later adulthood to old age: Smallpox, heart disease, cancer, rheumatism/arthritis, diseases of the nervous system. Still also tuberculosis and venereal disease.

X Across all age-groups: Influenza, diarrhoea/enteritis, pneumonia/bronchitis, meningitis.

If you managed the first few months of life and then survived the virulent childhood diseases, you went on to 'enjoy' illnesses which killed many in their prime of life. These left many widows/widowers and fatherless/motherless children, often in poverty. Finally in older age you could suffer from ailments as a consequence of increased life expectancy or from the complexities and strains of modern society rather than from good old viruses - these are often referred to as *'social'* or *'lifestyle'* diseases.

Chronological time

The history of health and disease is about conquering or controlling many of these diseases. The period from 1900 to 1950 reflects this. The earlier years to about 1920 were associated with the late Victorian era through frequent epidemics especially of diseases of infancy and childhood. The inter-war years saw the eradication of many of them, with the exception of TB. By the later 1930's these were 'replaced' by other and different ailments, mainly of late adulthood and old age, which have become a feature of mid and later 20th century society.

The next sections look at the main diseases within each of the age-groups and how they affected Leicester.

Infant mortality: "Suffer the little children"

Nascentes moruntur finis que ob origine pendet

"Even as they spring into life they are dying, and their end depends upon their origin"

With such an epitaph, J. Wyatt Crane, one Leicester's earliest Medical Officers described one of the most tragic aspects of Leicester's public health history - its record of infant mortality. Leicester had one of the highest and most persistent levels of infant mortality in the country, a situation stretching back to the late 1870's. By the 1930's these high levels had fallen but it was only by the late 1940's that it could be said that the battle had been finally won!

'Infant mortality' refers to the number of infants who die shortly after birth, usually expressed as the number of infant deaths under 12 months per 1000 registered births in a given year (see Appendix A).

Five notifiable diseases and disabilities accounted for most infant deaths - summer diarrhoea, convulsions, lung diseases, atrophy/debility and premature births. The first three were regarded as preventable and curable but the other two were more intractable. The other cause of death was the overlying of infants, usually by mothers. Infants also died from diseases such as whooping cough, scarlet fever and diphtheria.

Lung diseases, mainly pneumonia and bronchitis, were usually a consequence of one of the other ailments especially summer diarrhoea,

Permanent and visible evidence of infant mortality

atrophy and debility.

Atrophy and debility were often grouped together as a catch-all for a wide range of disabilities. Atrophy is the wasting of part of the body, often but not necessarily apparent at the time of birth. It was sometimes referred to as *'marasmus'*. Debility refers to a more general 'failure to thrive' and could arise from the condition of atrophy but it was just as likely to be a product of the general health and environment of the child and family.

Convulsions are nervous spasms of an extreme form that may lead to death. These can be of a cerebral origin but in infants they were a consequence of a physical disease, for example extreme diarrhoea could cause a convulsion, or they were brought on by fevers including diphtheria, scarlet fever etc., contracted in the early months of infancy.

The meaning of premature birth is readily apparent and could have its origins in defects either in the unborn infant and/or the mother. Included in this would be still-births and miscarriages.

Summer diarrhoea tended to attract greater attention from the public health and medical authorities. It was the most persistent and virulent cause of infant deaths and there was an epidemic most years, notably in summer. As a bacterial or virus infection it was related to a range of similar ailments - dysentery, typhus etc. - which affected the wider population, especially in crowded urban areas and which had a common source - poor sanitation.

In 1893, the infant mortality rate per 1000 births was 220, a record worse than towns such as Liverpool, Manchester and Salford which had always been regarded as the ultimate 'sewers' in public health terms. In 1900, 1083 infants under the age of 12 months died in Leicester, a mortality rate of 174 which was already a marked improvement over the previous years. Nevertheless these accounted for 29% of *all* deaths in Leicester.

The situation improved dramatically if erratically over the years prior to the First World War. A record low of 863 infant deaths was achieved in 1905. This still accounted for 28% of total deaths although the infant mortality rate had at last fallen temporarily below 150.

During and immediately after the war, the figures show considerable fluctuations. There was a dramatic fall in infant deaths from 596 in 1915 to a new low of 351 in 1918, a fall of over 40% and the rate fell from 123 to 108. In 1919 it fell to below the magic figure of 100 for the first time (98) only to rise again to a renewed peak of 528 deaths in 1920, though the rate continued to fall. These fluctuations were attributed to population and other changes due to the war.

The period during the 1920's and 30's was generally one of real and sustained improvement although the infant mortality rates showed odd short-lived reversals, e.g. 1929, 1933, and 1937. Such was the improvement that in 1930 Leicester was now the fifth *best* town amongst the 38 towns in England and Wales (excluding London and its surrounding towns) with a population over 100,000. It was not until 1938 that the infant mortality rate fell below 50 per 1000 births.

The Second World War and its immediate aftermath saw further fluctuations - in two years infant deaths rose from their lowest level ever of 268 in 1944 to a renewed peak of 304 in 1946, but then fell away as dramatically to 121 in 1949. This was reflected in the infant mortality rates, 54 in 1946 but 24 by 1949, the lowest in Leicester's history. The post-war rise, whilst small by comparison with previous times, caused concern amongst medical and welfare authorities after their struggle to develop infant welfare provision during the previous two decades.

Summer diarrhoea had been the most persistent cause of infant deaths, but in 1902 the Medical Officer of Health argued that Leicester's terrible reputation in terms of all deaths from diarrhoea was no longer justified. In terms of infant deaths this was to a large extent valid. After a remarkable fall between 1900 and 1902 there was a resurgence to a peak of 277 summer diarrhoea deaths in 1904 (over 28% of infant deaths). This was followed by further but lower peaks in 1906, 1911 and 1921. Summer diarrhoea thereafter was not the major cause of infant deaths although there was an inexplicable and short-lived peak in 1944.

In the case of lung disease, deaths from this cause rocketed from 233 in 1900, to 411 in 1902, a rise of 76%, but then fell away as rapidly to 94 in 1905. There does not seem to be an explanation for this. Thereafter the levels fluctuated between 50 and 125 through to 1930, when it fell to 14 and to below 10 in 1938. As with diarrhoea there was a sudden but short-lived peak at the end of the Second World War. The pattern of frequent fluctuations may be related to other diseases in which pneumonia and bronchitis was the actual cause of death.

Greater progress was made in the case of convulsions. After a peak of 130 in 1901, deaths fell to just under 15 in 1917. Despite some temporary rises, including a significant peak in 1928, convulsions as a cause of death was effectively eliminated by the late 1930's.

The same pattern emerges in the case of atrophy and debility although with different timings. At the beginning of the century there had been a peak. Despite a further but lower peak in 1910 the numbers fell dramatically to the lowest recorded number in 1918 (39). Following a renewed peak in 1920 (80 deaths) the levels fell away and from 1932 the annual number was below 10, atrophy and debility had been eliminated as a cause of death.

The efforts to reduce premature deaths were less successful although increasing attention was given to this stubborn problem. The improvements in the other diseases and ailments were the result of advances in welfare and public health provision. The causes of premature deaths are different and were less understood. The levels of deaths remained well above 100 deaths per year until the outbreak of the Great War, with peaks of over 150. There was a marked decline during the war to a low of just over 60 in 1919, which was related to changes in the birth rate. By 1920 numbers had returned to pre-war levels. During the 1920's and 1930's levels of deaths whilst significantly lower nevertheless remained high. There was a renewed peak in 1946. It was only from 1950 onwards that real advances were made to reduce but not to eradicate such deaths.

Why were levels of infant mortality so persistently high in Leicester? A number of inter-related factors were put forward to explain not only the levels of infant mortality but also the specific causes.

An early suggestion was that there was a link between infant mortality rates and the birth rates. Earlier reports of the Medical Officers had suggested that high infant mortality rates would actually lead to higher birth rates. Dr Charles Killick Millard, Medical Officer of Health for Leicester from 1901, cited one of his predecessors:

*"It is certain that a great fatality among infants in any town will tend to raise the birth rate, for the mothers who lose their infants early become in a short time pregnant again. From this I am disposed to regard the high birth rate in Leicester as a natural consequence of the excessive infant mortality." **(MOH 1904)***

Reductions in infant mortality prior to the First World War coincided with those in the birth rate (see Appendix B), suggesting a relationship between the two although its exact nature was complex.

During the Great War there was a huge fall in the birth rate and also in infant mortality. The actual causes were the consequences of the war itself. Dr Millard and others could not understand this which was contrary to previous explanations:

*"When it is considered that so many mothers are at work and away from home the greater part of the day, and that in consequence very many more infants have had to be put out to nurses than was the case in pre-war times, this reduction in infant mortality is all the more remarkable. There is, however, one consideration to be borne in mind. Owing to the increased number of marriages on the one hand, and the absence of husbands on the other, an unduly large proportion of the births now occurring must, we may argue, be the result of recent marriages. In other words they are 'first babies' and 'first babies' usually come in for more care and attention than those which arise in families already 'over-run' with children, and whose advent, in many cases, is not particularly desired. Still another consideration is that the mothers in these cases are often earning abnormally high wages and, in the case of soldiers' wives, are also in receipt of the separation allowances, so that poverty - that arch-enemy of infant life and one of the most fruitful causes of infant mortality - has been comparatively rare..." **(MOH 1916)***

A later report further confused the matter: *"...But much of this exceptional decline which occurred during the war was due, without doubt, to the absence from the country of so many potential fathers. Such children as were born, therefore, were to a large extent begotten by men left behind. But the men left behind were certainly inferior from the point of view of physical health to the men sent* *to the front. We should certainly have anticipated, then, that the children begotten by them would have been below the average in vitality, and that this fact alone would have led to higher infant mortality. That infant mortality has fallen instead of risen is, therefore, all the more satisfactory, even though we are unable to explain it." **(MOH 1919)***

Such shifts during the Second World War were at a much lower scale and did not follow the same course as the Great War. Infant mortality numbers actually rose slightly during the war itself to a marked peak in 1946 with a more rapid and steeper rise in births to a final peak in 1947.

The report of 1916 placed emphasis upon poverty as a major factor in infant mortality. Undoubtedly the highest incidence was amongst the poorer sections of society. Low wages, often combined with frequent unemployment and unemployability, led to a low standard of living and a poor diet (with food often adulterated). Thus ill-fed and unhealthy mothers often working on low wages, remaining in work until late into pregnancies and returning soon after, would be likely to give birth to weakly infants, usually into an already large family. If they did not die within weeks (the incidence of mortality within the first six or so weeks of life was particularly high) they would succumb to many of the ailments associated with infant mortality.

This is an over-simplification. Poverty was not just a cause but as much a symptom of other major causes, the most significant being poor sanitation and housing. Poor people lived in the most densely populated parts of Leicester. The overcrowded houses were often badly maintained with inadequate water and toilet provision, with few facilities for the safe storage of food and with poor ventilation for the many large families. Some parts of the town such as St Margarets and All Saints had a long legacy of poor sanitation given their location in the lower and industrial areas along the River Soar. Not surprisingly the infant mortality rates were high as were the mortality rates for a number of childhood and adult diseases.

Likewise poverty was both a factor and a symptom of wider inter-related social factors - poor maternity and mothercraft skills, ignorance, depravity and social class. Poverty brought not just physical deprivation but also social deprivation. This included limited access to health and welfare facilities and limited money to meet the costs of them. Again, this applied across the full range of mortality and not to just infant mortality:

*"...It is a well-known fact that social conditions have a great influence upon birth and death rate. At the top of the social scale people live longer, have smaller families, and such children as are born have a much better chance of surviving. At the bottom of the social scale the reverse holds good." **(MOH 1924)***

On the issue of ignorance and social class, the Medical Officer cites a national report:

"...Maternal ignorance is sometimes regarded as a chief factor in the causation of excessive child mortality. It is a comfortable doctrine for the well-to-do to adopt; and it goes far to relieve his conscience in the contemplation of excessive suffering and mortality amongst the poor... There is little reason to believe that the average ignorance in matters of health of the working-class is much

*greater than that of mothers in other classes of society..." **(MOH 1916)***

The report noted that well-to-do mothers have time to spend on their infants or have help, good conditions for keeping the baby's food, adequate medical and other help and the means to 'overcome' their initial ignorance. By comparison, the poorer mother has to look after many children and her husband, do the housekeeping, has no pantry, little medical or other help and little opportunity to overcome her ignorance.

The issue of high infant mortality in Leicester had been recognised by successive Medical Officers of Health. Its eradication became a crusade for Dr Millard, the Medical Officer of Health, throughout his long period of service in Leicester from 1901 until 1935 and was continued by his successor Dr MacDonald.

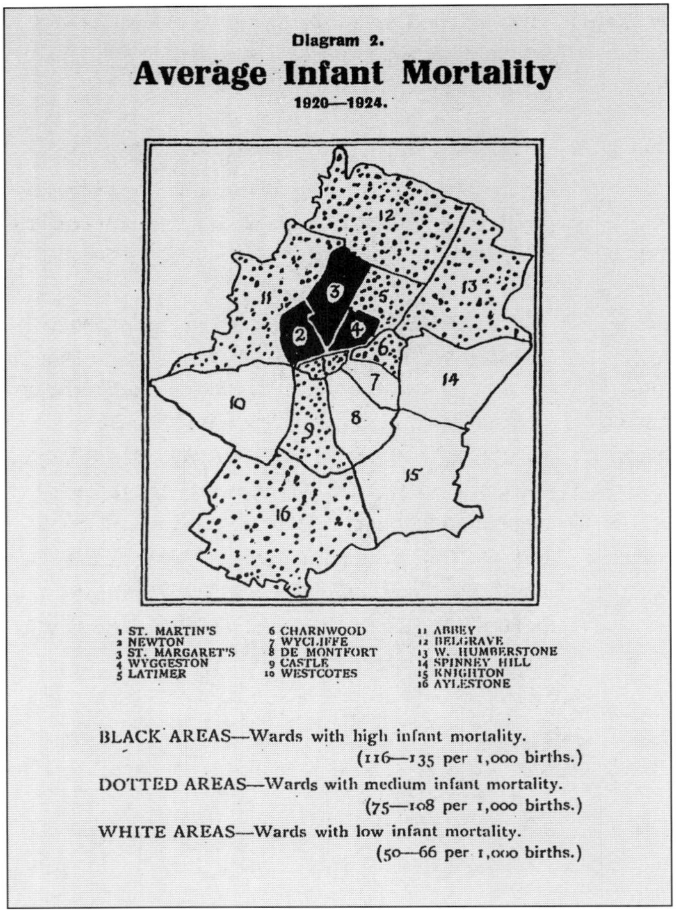

There were three broad avenues pursued by the public health authorities - physical environmental improvements, welfare provision and medical advancement. The first two were central to public health and it was in these that the greatest progress was made. Less progress was made on the third as any advances in medical science were not determined by public health.

Environmental improvements prior to the Great War had been mainly in public sanitation and were not directed specifically towards infant mortality. Most of the actual improvements had taken place in the later years of the 19th century and we saw their fuller impact during the earlier years of the 20th century. These included improvements in water supply and the completion of the conversion to flush toilets. These were major factors in reducing infant mortality.

The most important development was in the field of infant and maternal welfare. Changes had begun before the Great War - the opening of the Milk Depot in 1906, training of midwives,

Diagram 2.

Average Infant Mortality

1920—1924.

1 ST. MARTIN'S
2 NEWTON
3 ST. MARGARET'S
4 WYGGESTON
5 LATIMER
6 CHARNWOOD
7 WYCLIFFE
8 DE MONTFORT
9 CASTLE
10 WESTCOTES
11 ABBEY
12 BELGRAVE
13 W. HUMBERSTONE
14 SPINNEY HILL
15 KNIGHTON
16 AYLESTONE

BLACK AREAS—Wards with high infant mortality. (116—135 per 1,000 births.)

DOTTED AREAS—Wards with medium infant mortality. (75—108 per 1,000 births.)

WHITE AREAS—Wards with low infant mortality. (50—66 per 1,000 births.)

Medical Officer of Health report, 1924

expansion of the work of health visitors and the opening of ante-natal clinics. The pace and nature of these and other developments increased greatly in the 1920's and 1930's - notably the opening of the Westcotes Maternity Hospital in 1920, the wider and more extensive development of ante- and post-natal and child welfare clinics and nursery provision. Shirley Aucott in her book '*Mothercraft and Maternity*' provides an excellent account of these developments.

Such developments were primarily preventative although the concept of 'prevention' widened to embrace health and maternity education. This extended into the field of school education especially through hygiene classes for older girls. The Education Act of 1918 with its curriculum provisions may have helped in this. The other innovation was the introduction of birth control advice, albeit limited to married women already with children. It was through such developments that the issue of ignorance was challenged.

Regardless of these efforts and the dramatic improvement in infant mortality levels in Leicester, Dr Millard still believed that infant mortality could be virtually eradicated:

"Whilst we cannot expect to bring down the general death rate below a certain point, seeing that everyone must die some day, there is no theoretical limit below which infant mortality may not fall, since infants are born to live, not to die, and it is not really necessary that any infant should die during the first year of life...

"...At the same time, until we know more about the influences at work before birth (ante-natal factors) and how to control them, it is too much to expect that infant mortality will ever be entirely eliminated. A large number of infants are really sentenced to death before they are born, and when they are born so handicapped in one respect or another that they are physically unable to maintain the battle of life under the fundamentally altered conditions of their environment."
(MOH 1927)

Dr Millard's crusade was successful. By 1949, after his retirement, Leicester's terrible reputation which he had inherited had been reversed and his successor Dr MacDonald could proudly declare:

"...It is therefore all the more gratifying for me to be able to report that this year (1949) Leicester has not only achieved the lowest infant mortality rate in its history viz., 23.8 per 1,000 live births, but occupies the proud position of holder of the lowest infant mortality rate of any of the twenty largest towns in this country... At this figure, we must be approaching the 'irreducible minimum' as it is called, but while one infant life is lost through preventable causes, we must feel that there is still room for improvement." ***(MOH 1949)***

Infancy and childhood

This section looks at four highly infectious and virulent childhood diseases - diphtheria, measles, scarlet fever and whooping cough, all inherited from the previous century.

Until the late 1940's there continued to be a high incidence of all four diseases with frequent though declining epidemics, with fortunately declining numbers of deaths. Because these diseases were so common, many parents regarded them as 'normal' and failed to realise that while the possibility of death became remote, there could still be deaths from related illnesses and long term, or permanent effects. This impeded efforts to eradicate the diseases.

Diphtheria

Diphtheria is now effectively unknown in this country, although it is still prevalent in the rest of the world. Your local doctor might have difficulty in recognising it. Only people in their fifties or over are likely to remember it as a particularly dangerous childhood disease:

"I caught diphtheria. My family came to Leicester from the north of England in January 1938. We

lived in Brazil Street, a most respectable street occupied mostly by professional people. All was well until Whitsuntide of 1939. We had been back north for the weekend. A few days later I fell ill with a sore throat which quickly became a fever. The doctor suspected diphtheria and I was hurried off to Groby Road Isolation Hospital. I became seriously ill for some days, going temporarily blind and deaf, fortunately not needing a tracheotomy.

"In those days there was a glass case outside the City Health Department offices in Grey Friars which listed the condition of all those hospital patients suffering from diphtheria and similar acute diseases. I was on the list.

"Back at home all my toys were put in my bedroom, the room was then sealed, fumigated and stoved. My parents had to have throat swabs, but my sister had been immunised. Immunisation had been introduced into Leicester just a few years before.

"My family visited me but they saw me through the windows. I was in hospital for several weeks, certainly until a few days after my fifth birthday at the beginning of July. I was still physically very thin and weak, and for some weeks I had go out in a pushchair. I missed the beginning of the school term.

"How did I come to catch diphtheria? At first it was thought it had been through ice-cream eaten whilst on holiday. However, discussions between my parents indicated another source, the actual one. I had been with my sister to her friend's house in the next street and I had played on a large wooden toy in the next door garden. Unknown to my parents, but revealed on enquiry, the boy at that house had recently been taken to hospital with diphtheria! I had not been immunised as I had only briefly attended school in Leicester. So I caught the disease via a toy. I was lucky as many children of my age would have died." **(CH, then nearly 5)**

This is a typical account of the nature and spread of diphtheria. It is a highly contagious and virulent bacterial disease. Initial symptoms are a sore throat, hard cough and fever. One of its life threatening dangers is the blocking of the air passage which sometimes requires surgical measures. There could be temporary deafness and blindness.

The disease dates back early in medical history and was particularly prevalent during the 19th century, culminating in a major epidemic in the 1890's which affected Leicester. The medical cause of the disease was known quite early although the conditions affecting its spread were disputed well into this century:

"Diphtheria is a most elusive disease, which is endemic rather than epidemic in this country, that it to say, it is continually present in every large centre of population, and the numbers of fresh cases occurring year by year, whilst there are considerable fluctuations, does not amount, as a rule, to what is usually understood as an epidemic." **(MOH 1933)**

Although stressing the seriousness of diphtheria, it is significant that in Leicester the numbers of deaths had already fallen dramatically by 1904 and was effectively controlled, if not quite eradicated, as a major killer disease. Unlike measles and scarlet fever this was achieved primarily through medical advances - starting with the development and use of diphtheria antitoxin and culminating in the 1930's with immunisation as a means of protection and prevention.

The century opened with Leicester at the height of a major diphtheria epidemic. There were 1452 notified cases and 316 deaths in 1900 - a mortality rate of 22%. The number of cases fell inexplicably over the next four years to reach a low of 9 in 1904, a figure not repeated until 1949. In between there were regular peaks in the number of cases but which did not necessarily qualify as true epidemics - 1920, 1925, 1930, 1935, 1938 and a final high peak in 1940 - roughly a five year cycle. However, deaths were generally under 20 per year except in 1920, 1938 and 1940 (42, 33 and 50 cases respectively). 1940 was the last significant epidemic with 840 notified cases.

If you caught diphtheria, you were immediately sent to Groby Road Isolation Hospital. Two injections of diphtheria antitoxin (at most, three doses) was the main and virtually only means of combating the disease. Along with this was nursing treatment - the clearing and irrigating of the nose and throat and use of antiseptic lotions. Surgery was carried out only in acutely life threatening cases - tracheotomy and the insertion of a tube to allow breathing:

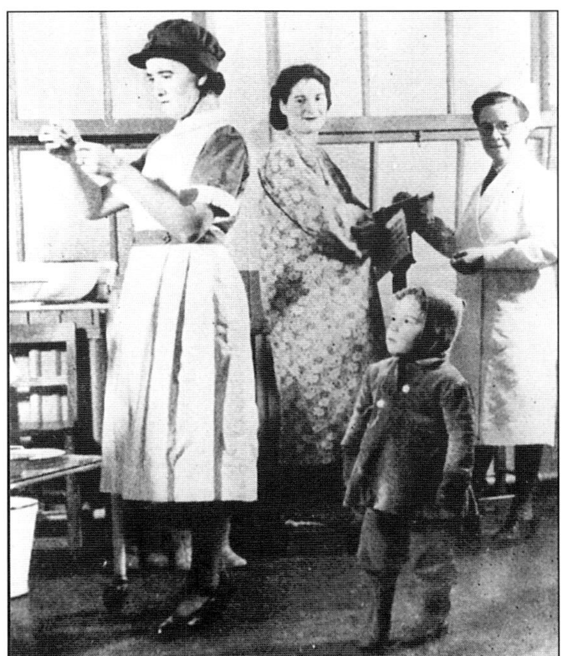

Getting your diphtheria injection! (c.1940's)

"One case in particular I noticed, where the child had been ill twenty four hours before removal to hospital, and almost moribund on admission, was injected with 2000 units of Antitoxin, and fed with brandy and beef-tea at half-hourly intervals. Within twenty four hours the patient wanted to sit up." ***(MOH 1900)***

For most cases, the antitoxin worked but excessive use of it along with the use of alcohol (brandy or whisky) could give rise to heart problems. The use of alcohol was discontinued at Groby Road Isolation Hospital in 1910.

There was frequent discussion of the environmental factors in the cause and spread of the disease and of possible means of containing it. It was assumed that the incidence of diphtheria would be higher in the more crowded poorer areas of the town and linked to the insanitary conditions. This was not entirely so:

"In all houses where diphtheria occurs the drains are tested with the smoke test. Defects are not infrequently detected, the escape of gas is nearly always external to the house. It is doubtful whether drain defects have as much to do with the causation of this disease as is often supposed. The mere presence of slight drainage faults is not of much significance as they are found to exist in a great many old houses. Moreover, the disease

*frequently occurs in comparatively new houses where the conditions of the drains is apparently quite satisfactory..." **(MOH 1914)***

By 1924 the question seemed to be resolved:

*"The disease has been attributed to dampness, to characters of the subsoil, to rainfall, and to fluctuations in level of ground water, to drainage defects, and to insanitation generally. To-day the commonly accepted view is that the disease is due to a specific organism, the diphtheria bacillus, and is spread from person to person largely through unrecognised cases, much as the cases with other infectious diseases, and that certain obscure 'epidemic influences' promote and enhance the vitality and virulence of the Diphtheria bacillus from time to time, leading to epidemic prevalence of the disease." **(MOH 1924)***

The significance of 'person to person' contact had been recognised nearly twenty five years previously:

"Instructions were also given that slates were to be cleaned with a sponge instead of by the usual school-boy way of licking: slate pencils, pens etc., were disinfected before being used in class; drinking cups, which are in frequent use during warm weather were removed from the taps; and the children made to understand that when one of them became the proud possessor of one of those large hard lumps of sugar (I regret I do not know the technical name but I think that they go by the common term of 'bulls-eyes') the said lump was not to be passed round the immediate circle of friends, so that all might enjoy the flavour."
(MOH 1900)

By the mid 1920's the main issue in Leicester concerning diphtheria was that of immunisation. The vaccine had reached a stage where it had been used in Edinburgh and in parts of London. Dr Millard was very sceptical with regard to it ostensibly on the grounds of its *'value and practicality'*, but underlying this was his belief that immunisation would not be accepted in Leicester given the long controversy dating back to 1870 over smallpox inoculation. (This controversy is outlined in a later section on the smallpox epidemic of 1903-4):

*"...In Leicester it is probable that many parents would at first object on principle to their children being inoculated , but as it would be entirely optional and subject to the parents' consent, without any question of compulsion, objection to it would doubtless disappear in time if it could really be shown to be of value..." **(MOH 1925)***

Dr Millard continued to accept the seriousness of the disease but still doubted the likely effect of immunisation and anticipated resistance to it by the public until his retirement in 1935. His successor, Dr MacDonald, was not restricted by this and in 1935 suggested that hospitalisation of diphtheria patients had not been an effective preventative measure and that there was now enough evidence to show that immunisation did protect the individual and the community. He put forward plans for an immunisation programme in Leicester. This was introduced over the next two years without the public resistance his predecessor had predicted.

It was successful but in 1950 he was alarmed at a decline in numbers of children being immunised. This was due to concern amongst some members of the public over rumoured links between immunisation and polio:

"...If this continues, it will be tragic, and parents must take warning. One of the reasons for this loss of public confidence has undoubtedly been due to the publicised connection between infantile paralysis and hyperdermic injection... It would be absolute foolishness to refuse immunisation because of the risk of contracting infantile paralysis - the most that need be done is to postpone the immunisation procedure till infantile paralysis is no longer epidemic - i.e a month or so - and it's very doubtful whether even this is wise. Unchecked diphtheria is a far greater peril than infantile paralysis." ***(MOH 1950)***

He was right!

Measles

Measles still remains one of the most virulent childhood illnesses having both short term effects such as pneumonia, but more devastating long term and permanent effects including eye damage and even blindness. As scarlet fever declined measles 'took over' as a major childhood disease.

Parents never fully recognised its seriousness - a constant cause for concern on the part of Leicester's public health authorities:

"There is undoubtedly a tendency amongst the poor to treat measles too lightly, as if it were a trifling complaint. 'Only measles' is a common expression. Scarlet Fever, though not a more fatal disease, is regarded with much more respect." ***(MOH 1909)***

How prevalent was measles in Leicester? We have numbers of deaths but not of cases as it was not a notifiable disease until 1938. There is evidence of a high and persistent incidence of the disease through to and beyond 1950. Unlike scarlet fever, measles did not just 'go away'!

There were regular epidemics of measles of varying scale every three years or so until about 1920. There was an epidemic in 1902-03 and the previous one had been in 1898. The 1908-09 was the worst one for ten years and was the last one of such a scale, when there were 124 deaths in an eight week period. There were 167 deaths in 1908, of which 160 were children under 5 years of age and 34 under 1 year. This was followed by a further 109 deaths early in 1909. Further epidemics followed - in 1911 (relatively minor) and 1916-17 (8379 cases with more than 140 deaths).

Thereafter, the outbreaks appeared about every 4 years. There was an increase in deaths but not an epidemic in 1920, a minor one in 1925 (44 deaths) followed by minor outbreaks and a gratifying decline in deaths to under 10 per year from 1935. However, there was a further series of outbreaks of epidemic proportions in rapid succession - culminating in 1940 with 5878 notified cases, far greater than scarlet fever (1315 cases), diphtheria (840 cases) and whooping cough (306 cases). Such high numbers of cases were repeated in 1945 (5493) and in 1949 (4195).

It is not surprising given the nature of the disease, that its incidence and mortality was greatest amongst the poor sections of the population who lived in the older crowded parts of Leicester.

The public health authorities attempted to reduce both the prevalence and mortality in two ways - isolation, and school closure and exclusion. Isolation presented problems:

"Isolation may be attempted at home or in hospital. In the homes of the poor isolation is usually impracticable, and the difficulty is increased by the fact that in many cases at the end of a few days the child appears convalescent and is difficult to keep in bed. Isolation in hospital may be useful as a means of preventing the spread of the disease during the early stages of an outbreak, and valuable as a means of reducing mortality. Unfortunately, measles is highly infectious in the pre-eruptive stage, at the beginning of an attack before the rash appears. During this time the symptoms are very much those of an ordinary feverish cold, and thus notification or precautionary measure are delayed." ***(MOH 1917)***

Isolation for poorer large families in crowded houses was particularly difficult:

"...with a large family in a small house and with limited means, it is often very difficult to give the same care and attention that is possible and easy under more favourable circumstances. In many cases of measles the child is treated on the couch downstairs, more or less exposed to draughts, partly for convenience and partly to save extra fire." ***(MOH 1909)***

Hospital isolation was never the practice for measles as with scarlet fever, diphtheria and smallpox due to the greater number of cases.

Schools were recognised as a major breeding ground and closure was adopted in the earlier years of the period, but it came to be regarded as being ineffective. There was an inordinately long period from the very first case to the last especially in large families. Exclusion became the practice and there were rules set down by Leicester's School Medical Officer:

"1. Children recovering from measles are not allowed to return to school for ***four weeks*** *from the time they were first taken ill.*

2. Other children in the same house, not themselves suffering the disease, are divided into two categories:
(a) Those in the Infants' Department, or in Standard I and II.
(b) Those in Standard III and upwards.
Classes (a) are kept from school for two weeks after the onset of the last cases.
Classes (b), if they already had the disease (and a great majority of children have), are allowed to continue attendance at school."

(MOH 1909)

It was recognised that there were other situations which brought children together. There was an interesting discussion in the health report in 1917 on the effect of a new leisure phenomenon - the picture theatre - on the spread of disease:

"...The picture theatre, especially where children's performances are held, obviously constitutes a real danger as far as the spread of infectious disease is concerned. The arrangement for such performances in Leicester are that a charge of one penny only is made, and the entertainment lasts for two hours on Saturday afternoons. They are greatly patronised, and the picture theatres are sometimes filled to their utmost seating capacity, as many as 1000 or 1600 children being crowded together as close as they can sit..." ***(MOH 1917)***

A solution was proposed and forwarded to the Watch Committee responsible for the licensing of cinemas:

"...to consider the practicality of duplicating children's performances, and at the same time reducing the duration of the performance and the number of children allowed to be present at a time by one half. As one hour's entertainment for one penny is still extremely good value, it is unlikely that the total attendance would be materially affected, so that the proprietors should not suffer financially and but little extra trouble would be involved. A short interval between the performances should be insisted upon, during which the building could be thoroughly aired."
(MOH 1917)

There is no record of the outcome!

Efforts were made to change attitudes of parents, especially mothers, with regard to the dangers of measles and what should be done when a child became a victim. In the earlier years this was through the display of notices in public places but the development of maternal and child welfare clinics was to become a more effective method. Improvements in housing, sanitation and hygiene became the most effective long term means of reducing the incidence of the disease.

The only real treatment was to nurse the child through the worst stages:

"I would like to point out that the method of treating measles in this hospital is by nursing such cases, warmly clad, in the open air as far as possible day and night. This is in marked contrast to the procedure usually adopted in outside practice, where such cases are often kept in the hot, stuffy atmosphere of an almost hermetically sealed room with a large fire burning in the grate."
(Report of Superintendent of the Isolation Hospital and Sanatorium 1923)

In the home there was recourse to cough remedies, tonics and, for some reason aperients (laxatives!).

BOROUGH OF LEICESTER.

MEASLES.

Measles is a ***very serious disease.***

It causes more deaths than Smallpox, Scarlet Fever, and Typhoid Fever put together.

Most of the deaths are in young children under the age of 3 or 4 years.

There is a special reason, therefore, for striving to protect children from it during the early years of life.

SYMPTOMS.

These at first suggest an ordinary feverish cold—sneezing, coughing, running at eyes and nose, &c ; occasionally vomiting, diarrhœa, or shivering. The ***rash*** usually does not appear till third or fourth day, is red and spotty in character, and is present on face and neck as well as on body and limbs.

The disease ***is very infectious*** from the very beginning, so if measles is suspected the case should be ***isolated at once*** in a room by itself. When this is not possible, at least keep it away from the younger children who have not had the disease.

NURSING.

Keep child warm ***in bed*** ; avoid exposure to draught ; keep room at even temperature. Burn all discharges from mouth, nose or eyes. Feed on milk and slops. The chief danger lies in catching a chill. The child should be carefully sponged over with warm water every day.

INFECTION.

In slight cases children may appear well at end of 10 days, but they must be treated as still infectious and not be allowed out until end of third week. At termination of case, ***wash everything*** that can be washed and thoroughly air everything else.

SCHOOL ATTENDANCE.

Children ***in Standard III and upwards***, if they have already had the disease, need not be kept from school. All others must be kept away until two weeks after the beginning of the last case.

Children recovering from Measles must not be sent to school for at least four weeks (counting from the first day of being taken ill).

Notice issued by Medical Officer of Health, 1908

Scarlet Fever

Scarlet fever was one of the most virulent and persistent illnesses with frequent epidemics and inevitable deaths, and prior to 1900 there had been epidemics in Leicester in 1893-4 and 1896. After 1910, although there were further epidemics through to the late 1930's, the number of deaths had declined. In 1901 Leicester's Medical Officer of Health had suggested that scarlet fever was no longer the scourge that it had been:

"It has now become a comparatively trifling complaint, probably less fatal than Measles. To what this beneficent change in type is attributable is not known. It is thought by some to be only a passing phase, and that a return to the old severe type may at any time occur. There is not, fortunately, any evidence of this taking place at present, on the other hand, the tendency in most places is towards a still lower fatality. Simultaneously, the proportion of serious complications and sequelae has been greatly reduced, so that at the present time Scarlet Fever can scarcely be considered as one of our most important Zymotics." ***(MOH 1901)***

He was correct with regard to its declining severity but less so with regard to numbers of cases and deaths. For example, the number of scarlet fever cases rose from 500 in 1904 to a peak of 2300 in 1906, a rise of 460%, and 52 deaths - the last major epidemic. There were 44 and then 38 deaths in the next two years.

After 1915 there were really significant falls in numbers and deaths. There were further epidemics of varying but lesser intensity and duration of a milder scarlet fever in 1921, 1928 (a significant one with 1980 notified cases), 1934-35 and 1940. The number of deaths were under 5 per year except in 1922 and 1925 when there were 7 and 10 respectively.

Normally, scarlet fever patients were placed in isolation in Groby Road Isolation Hospital:

"The Isolation Hospital is so popular with the general public in Leicester that so far from there being any difficulty in inducing parents to allow their children to come to hospital, it is difficult rather to keep them out, even in cases where with a little trouble and inconvenience the patient might be nursed at home." ***(MOH 1908)***

During the smallpox epidemics of 1903-04 there was a severe shortage of hospital beds, so scarlet fever patients and others were sent home, no further patients were accepted and their isolation had to be at home. This did not lead to any significant increases in the incidence of the disease, in fact numbers were beginning to fall. By the 1930's as a result of this and subsequent experience hospital isolation in Leicester was no longer automatic, only the more serious and needy cases being admitted.

Isolation of patients in a separate room at home became routine but it presented problems in small houses with large families. The correct practice was to put up a disinfection curtain on the door of the isolation room, with continual disinfection of utensils, clothes etc. This was followed by obligatory disinfection and fumigation of the room and contents.

The incidence of the disease was always highest in the older crowded areas of the town. Controlling the spread of the disease in such areas was made more difficult as parents often allowed their infected patient to go into the streets and even to school after the initial fever had abated but yet still at the *'sequelae'* stage, that is, when they were very infectious with weeping open spots.

The decline of the disease was helped by greater awareness of this and the related complications of the disease, in particular post-scarlatina-diphtheria, and with the general improvements in hygiene, health and housing. The decline was not particularly due to advances in medicine, the only real treatment being warmth and good ventilation, baths and lotions, that is, good basic nursing.

Despite the long history of scarlet fever epidemics, the exact causes and workings of it still baffled the medical authorities and it is not entirely clear why the disease disappeared as a major killer.

Whooping cough

This childhood illness tended to be overlooked, as like measles it was *'only whooping cough!'* Yet it led directly to the deaths of quite a lot of children or indirectly, through related respiratory causes such as pneumonia, or convulsions due to coughing - the characteristic *'whoop'* - leading to rupture of the brain. The disease could last for ten or twelve weeks.

Until 1930 the annual death rates fluctuated erratically. The highest number of deaths was in 1906 - 112 deaths - a legacy of the previous century when it was a particularly virulent disease. There were significant peaks in 1910, 1914 and a final one in 1925. Thereafter, there was a more consistent downward trend.

The disease was not a notifiable one until its incidence had fallen to a relatively low point. It did not attract the attention of the Medical Officer as did the other diseases. Yet when they did make note of it, they stressed its seriousness:

"Measles, whooping cough, both non-notifiable infectious diseases, cause more deaths than do all the notifiable diseases together." ***(MOH 1902)***

In 1902 there were 68 whooping cough deaths, (39 under 1 year) and 78 measles deaths. There were 1044 notified cases but only 5 deaths in 1949.

"This is a much more important disease - it is unfortunate that a really satisfactory immunisation material is as yet not available though no doubt it will not be long before research is successful."
(MOH 1949)

In 1950 there were 961 notifiable cases and fortunately only 3 deaths:

"If only infection could be avoided till the child was older and thus more able to stand the disease, lives could be saved. Parents should take the utmost care to prevent a young baby from contact with a known case of whooping cough."
(MOH 1950)

Whooping cough is a bacterial airborne disease. It was inevitably difficult to control especially in dense housing areas and amongst large families. The fact that a child could still be infectious for many weeks was a particular complication. Parents were reprimanded for their carelessness in allowing their still infectious children to roam the streets or go to school. It was always regarded as being preventable and that good nursing could limit its effects, very difficult in poorer large families in overcrowded houses.

As with many of the other diseases there was no effective remedy. One home remedy consisted of a mixture of 'salts of tartar', cochineal and sugar or honey. The eventual answer was immunisation which was not introduced until after 1950.

There were many other infectious childhood diseases which did not attract as much attention but were ever present and a part of normal childhood. Whilst many were not necessarily fatal they could have longer term effects Diseases such as mumps, chickenpox and the most dangerous, German measles and meningitis, are still around today.

In addition there were a number of contagious ailments which, whilst not being specifically of childhood, tended to have a greater incidence amongst children having friends at school and at play, and their association with dirt. Ringworm was still present in the earlier years, scabies was serious enough to require the establishment of a special bathing station and impetigo was common. These were not life-threatening so did not always get the attention they deserved.

Leicester's health visitors, 1927

Adolescence, Adulthood and Older Age

Adolescence and adulthood

The major disease of adolescence and adulthood in Leicester during this period was tuberculosis. This requires a section of its own as does smallpox. Of the other diseases which particularly affected adolescent and younger adults only polio attracted public attention whereas dangerous ailments such as rheumatic fever and meningitis were largely ignored. The reasons for this are not clear.

Poliomyelitis

For most people poliomyelitis is a disease of early childhood hence its common name *'infantile poliomyelitis'*, but it affects older children, adolescents and even adults.

It is a distinctly cruel disease. Although most patients survive, the damaging effects are permanent and visible. Older readers may recall the summer of 1947, when an outbreak of the disease became an epidemic and they remember, and still know, school friends who were struck down by it. Some eventually returned to school permanently disabled.

It is an ancient viral disease affecting the nervous system which is transmitted through oral-faecal processes. Polio epidemics became more frequent towards the end of the 19th century. Ironically this was a product of the improvement in sanitation. Children and young adolescents had gained immunity naturally in early life but they had lost it, due to such improvements.

Between 1900 and 1950 there were nationally two epidemics in 1926 and 1947. This generated great anxiety in Leicester and elsewhere as in most years there was only the occasional death.

The most alarming feature of the disease is the suddenness of its onset and its course:

"Occasionally, a child may go to bed apparently well and be found next morning with a limb or limbs paralysed. Usually, however, the onset begins with a feverish attack which may last for two or three days or longer. This may be accompanied by one or more of the following symptoms: fretfulness, vomiting, retraction of the neck, pains in limbs, etc. Paralysis of one or more groups of muscles then supervenes. The parts usually affected are the leg, the foot, the arm, the shoulder, the back, occasionally the face. In bad cases both upper and lower limbs may be involved. Such cases as described above are usually easily recognised, but others are more indefinite and diagnosis may then be difficult. With the appearance of the paralysis the initial feverish attack usually passes off but the paralysis remains and may become permanent. Moreover, the nutrition of the affected limb is seriously interfered with, with the result that it may cease to grow and develop as it should do." ***(MOH 1926)***

Little was known of how the disease was spread. It was rare for a sick patient to infect a healthy person. Until the development much later of a vaccine, there was no known prevention or treatment and the disease had to take its course. Furthermore, as noted above, the initial symptoms could suggest only a minor feverish ailment and so delay diagnosis.

In the 1926 epidemic there were 81 notified cases and whilst there were fewer deaths (7 deaths) than previous outbreaks there was a greater degree of paralysis. The incidence of the disease was greatest amongst the very young. Thus 45 (56%) cases were under the age of 4 and 24 (30%) aged between 5 and 9 years of age. The split between sexes was 44 (54%) male and 37 (46%) female. Thirty of the cases were admitted to hospital. There was no specific pattern in the distribution of cases around the town or of a particular social group. The Medical Officer of Health noted the particular severity of the epidemic:

"The outbreak was quite an exceptional one, and there is no record of a similar one since the disease was made notifiable in the City, there was an outbreak in the County and, in proportion to population, about the same dimensions."
(MOH 1927)

The 1947 epidemic was regarded as the most severe one although there was only one death. There were 86 cases, of which 44 caused paralysis especially in the legs, the remaining 42 were described as *'abortive'*, that is without paralysis. The age incidence showed a marked shift to adolescence and early adulthood. Only 15 (17%) cases were under 4 years of age, and 29 (34%) aged between 5 and 14. The remaining 42 (nearly half) were aged over 15 and concentrated in the 15 - 24 and 25 - 34 age groups (21% and 16% respectively). The oldest case was a woman aged 53. As with the previous epidemic there was no discernible pattern in the social and spatial distribution of cases.

The epidemic began on 2 July, the highest number of cases peaked in the last two weeks of August with a further peak in mid-September. This concentration within the summer months was significant - it was considered that polio tended to be associated with hot, dry weather. That particular summer was hot and dry following the terrible winter of 1947. There was a further outbreak in 1949 with 51 cases and 2 deaths but the disease was a less severe form.

Vaccination of young children was introduced in the late 1950's and this could hopefully eradicate this cruel disease.

Venereal Disease

Venereal disease has a long history - it was first noted in Europe in the fifteenth century but goes back much further. It is a social disease but, because it is sexually transmitted, it is also a 'moral disease' which affects all social classes. Because of the relationship with social class and its well-known prevalence this 'scourge' was hidden and not discussed. As a consequence no concerted action was taken to combat it although a number of *'cures'* were used.

In his annual report for 1916 Dr Millard, Medical Officer of Health, departed somewhat from his normally guarded language:

"The year 1916 has been an epoch-making one in the history of venereal disease. Hitherto the policy

of silence and inaction has been followed as regards these diseases, which were regarded as outside the sphere of action of Public Health Authorities. Thanks, however, to the changing spirit of the times, aided by the Final Report of the Royal Commission and the splendid lead given by the Medical Department of the Local Government Board, the fiat has gone forth that the "hidden scourge" shall be hidden no longer. Henceforth, provided of course that the occasion is fitting, it will be permissible to discuss this question in public. It has been realised we cannot abolish an evil by the ostrich-like policy of shutting our eyes and pretending that it does not exist. The facts contained in the Royal Commission's Report have established the terrible character and widespread prevalence of the evil, and have brought home to the Country the importance of active measures being taken, without further delay, for dealing with it." ***(MOH 1916)***

There are underlying moral tones in this and later statements and that was in keeping with Dr Millard's fervent and long held views on social and moral matters.

In Leicester there was an immediate response to the report and a series of measures were put in place at an unprecedented speed. A meeting was held at the end of July 1916 attended by representatives of the town and county councils, the Leicester Royal Infirmary, medical practitioners, the Public Health authorities and the Local Government Board. The outcome was the establishment at the Leicester Royal Infirmary of out-patient Venereal Clinics for men and women, wards for in-patients and pathological services. Major H. Blakesley and Dr Bessie Symington were appointed to run the male and female clinics. They would also undertake home visits, where requested by medical practitioners. Drugs would be provided free of charge by the Leicester Corporation. The Board of Guardians made provision for treatment in the Poor Law Infirmary.

An educational programme of lectures and talks was organised, initially through the Local Branch of the National Council for Combating Venereal Disease. Such speed of action was almost certainly due to the open recognition of the horrors of VD:

"The whole subject of venereal disease is an inexpressibly sad and tragic one. It is the cause of an incalculable amount of injury to health, both individual and racial, injury which is far-reaching in its effects. In the case of the individual its worst effects are frequently not manifested till years after the disease has been contracted, and it may then attack the skin, the bones, the joints, the circulation, and worst of all the nervous system - indeed no part or tissue of the body is immune. Syphilis, indeed, is the most protean of all diseases, and gonorrhoea is only a little less serious. In addition to injury to physical health, venereal disease has serious psychological effects and is a most prolific cause of domestic misery and unhappiness." ***(MOH 1927)***

The scale of the problem had been unknown. In the first years of the clinic the recorded number of cases almost doubled - 593 (334 male, 259 female) in 1917, 719 (342 male, 377 female) in 1918 and 1163 (852 male, 311 female) in 1919. The ages of patients ranged from 9 to 70 years of age. Many had a long history of the disease and one was cited as having had it for 35 years. Patients were both married and single.

Some cases are cited:

"...26 years, single, stoker, has been attending clinic since 1919, with an interval of two years. Has had at least five courses of injections.

"...24 years single, motor driver, Gonorrhoea. This is his first attendance. Comes from the County with a letter from his doctor. Has had a severe attack and has been laid up in bed for six weeks with arthritis due to gonorrhoea. Is also suffering from iritis (form of inflammation of eye), and is at present unable to read...

"...an in-patient - an old man of 64 who came from a village in — . This was a very difficult case. The man was in a deplorable condition at the time of admission, and was suffering from both syphilis and gonorrhoea. There was very serious ulceration of the skull exposing the lining membrane of the brain. Had improved considerably since admission.

"...Woman of 31 - Looks a superior type. Is suffering from a serious complication of gonorrhoea (pyo-salpynx), which often necessitates a major operation (laparotomy).

"...Woman of 31 - Very bad perforation of the palate - 'speaks through the nose' - The bridge of the nose has also sunk, due to deep ulceration of the bones, causing serious disfigurement. Began treatment two years ago..." ***(MOH 1927)***

There was also concern about VD in children and babies. In young children it was transmitted through poor home hygiene such as dirty towels. In the case of babies it took a more serious form - *Ophthalmic Neonatorium:*

"As regards the cause of this very serious complaint, there is little doubt that the great majority of the more severe cases are due to gonorrhoeal infection derived from the mother at the time of birth. This is one of the most tragic aspects of the question of venereal disease, viz., the causation of permanent blindness in helpless infants." ***(MOH 1916)***

It is difficult to gauge the degree of success in the treatment of VD. We have no real measure of its incidence, of the attitude and behaviour of patients, the length of treatment required, especially in severe cases, and the tendency for many patients to stop attending clinics once the disease appeared to be stable These issues were recognised by the various medical officers responsible:

"The treatment and cure of Venereal Disease is as humiliating, tedious, expensive, and - from all points of view - a most unsatisfactory business. How infinitely better is prevention than cure; no other disease is more essentially preventable than venereal disease. If men and women could only be persuaded to abstain from certain actions there is every reason to believe that these loathsome complaints, would cease to exist. Though it may be Utopian to hope to abolish these entirely, whilst human nature is what it is, there is good reason to think that education on sex matters and enlightenment as to the dangers and risks involved by indulgence in promiscuous intercourse may do, and already has done, very much to minimise their ravages. Hence the great importance of appropriate propaganda." ***(MOH 1920)***

The VD Clinic was based in the Out-patients Department. There was considerable reluctance on the part of VD sufferers to attend the clinics on one afternoon and evening per week after the Out-patients Department had closed:

"Owing to the special nature of venereal disease there are very cogent reasons why the sufferers should avoid going to Clinics at public institutions, for in spite of the attempt made to keep the matter private and to suppress names, there must obviously be considerable risk to persons attending these clinics being recognised, either by the attendants, or by other patients." ***(MOH 1921)***

Consideration was given to making VD a notifiable disease but this was rejected:

"...such is the dread of publicity (and it is very natural it should be so) that many patients, if they knew that doctors had to notify, would certainly avoid seeking medical advice, much to their own detriment and that of the whole community. In the writer's opinion, the time does not yet seem ripe for such a step, whatever the future may have in store." ***(MOH 1922)***

Given the social nature of this preventable disease it was inevitable that the medical officers became increasingly involved in educational work. In schools there was the encouragement of sex hygiene amongst adolescent boys and girls. Talks in schools on sexual and moral issues by appropriate authorities were arranged, which were greatly appreciated by teachers, parents and pupils:

"...I find that only one girl was kept away by her parents from prejudice... On the other hand, the expressions of gratitude and approval from other parents are numerous. One lady told me that her daughter, aged 17, on returning home said, 'Mother, I had no idea it was all so wonderful', another girl wanted to tell her mother all about it and said she so much wanted to know still more. All the audience had the same attentive, reverent way of receiving the instruction that we noticed last year, and I could not discover the least sign of self-consciousness or foolishness."
(Letter from headmistress to MOH, 1920).

However, some people had moral objections to sex hygiene education outside the home:

"...think that sex is so personal, so sacred, and so intimately bound up with religion, that any systematic instruction, e.g. in a class of young people, is not only undesirable but improper."
(MOH 1927)

The medical and educational authorities recognised the sensitivity of such work and strictures were laid down concerning the *"dangers and pitfalls that beset them if certain rules of conduct are broken".*

In his 1930 report Doctor Millard returned to the problems of the sex urge - *"one of the strongest known to man"* and his 'Utopian hopes' with regard to morality and immorality. He divided men and women into three classes:

"1. Those who can be depended upon to 'keep straight' as the result of good upbringing and home training, or of innate rectitude of character.
2. Those who from weakness of character or otherwise will resort to illicit sex gratification, no matter what they are taught or told, provided the opportunity occurs.
3. An intermediate class whose fate is in the balance. Given good advice and a knowledge of the disastrous effects in the way of

permanent injury to health, which may result from promiscuous intercourse, this class may be influenced so as to avoid these dangers..." ***(MOH 1930)***

These are strong words. By 1930 considerable changes were taking place in society with regard to behaviour and the role and nature of marriage, including birth control:

"There is another method of combating VD which has been much more widely resorted to in certain continental countries than in this. This method, which is advocated by the Society for the Prevention of Venereal Disease, is based on the belief that we shall never be able to abolish promiscuity and that it is better to recognise this and to teach the individual how he can safeguard himself against the risk of infection when indulging in promiscuous relations.

"There are, however, two serious objections to this line of action. The first is the ethical objection which cannot be ignored or brushed aside.

"The other is the consideration that, whilst the immediate effect might be beneficial so far as the prevention of disease is concerned, the ultimate result might be just the reverse if - as might well be the case - it had the effect of encouraging promiscuity, because no methods of 'prevention' (i.e., safeguarding against infection) are entirely reliable. They are apt to break down when most required, and for this reason, if for no other, the writer is unable to feel much enthusiasm for the methods advocated by the Society referred to." ***(MOH 1930)***

What was originally a discussion of the prevention of VD clearly becomes one concerned with wider issues of sexual morality and human relationships. The tenor of the debates on these issues in these reports written in the 1920's and 30's is remarkably similar to debates in the 1960's on sexual freedom, *'free love', 'flower power'* etc., and the later more explosive debates in the 1980's arising from Aids.

Older Age

The two diseases of old age which attracted most attention were cancer and heart disease. Most of the diseases considered so far have shown a marked, even a dramatic decline and with some exceptions have become curable. These two show an entirely opposite trend. They were regarded at the time as largely non-preventable and incurable.

Rheumatism and arthritis, mainly diseases of old age, received scant attention possibly because they were merely changes of old age. Diseases such as Alzheimer's and Parkinson's Disease must have existed but were yet to be properly identified.

Cancer

Cancer is an ancient disease not a new one. Its increased incidence became apparent by the turn of the century. Public and medical health authorities began to give greater attention to it. Until relatively recently, within the wider community, the word *'cancer'* was spoken only in hushed tones.

Cancer was regarded as a disease of older age. Its increased incidence and mortality is, in part, a consequence of the reduction in mortality from diseases of younger age and in turn of the increased expectancy of life. It is now recognised that cancer is not confined to older age groups. It is also regarded as a product of changing lifestyle especially those aspects directly related to health.

The increase in cancer deaths was recognised by Leicester's Medical Officer of Health in 1908. He noted 214 cancer deaths in that year, representing 7% of total deaths and a mortality rate of 0.891 per 1000 population. Twenty years earlier the average number of deaths had been 75, 3% of total deaths, a rate of 0.486 per 1000 population. Leicester's position vis-à-vis other major towns was relatively good.

Between 1900 and 1950 the number of cancer deaths rose remorselessly, with only an odd year when figures fell, followed by a renewed upward surge. Such surges occurred in 1904, 1914, 1918, 1926 (a major increase), 1944 (no figures available for 1941, 1942 and 1943) and 1948. By 1948, cancer deaths had reached a then peak of 525. This gives a rate of 10% of total deaths and a mortality rate of 1.87 per 1000 population. It was now the second biggest killer after that other 'modern' disease, heart disease. Cancer was never a notifiable disease and therefore we have no figures for the true number of cases.

More attention was eventually given to cancer in the Medical Officer's reports. They show an increasing frustration and regret that cancer was an appalling and fearful disease, that little was known of its nature, that it could not be prevented and that there seemed to be no cure:

"Naturally this alarming fact, for which no satisfactory explanation has hitherto been adduced, gives cause for much uneasiness. Probably no disease is more dreaded, especially after middle age is reached, than is that which we are now considering. The very fact that a person is suffering from cancer is mentioned by his friends almost with bated breath. It is unnecessary to dwell here upon the long drawn out misery and suffering which death from malignant disease so often implies. As regards to hope of recovery, few genuine cases do appear to get well spontaneously, or at least to become quiescent, but such cases are extremely rare. The vast majority of cases pass on to a final termination...

"...As to the cause of cancer it is deeply to be regretted that the etiology of the disease is still most obscure. All sorts of theories have been put forward as to its causation, but none of these, so far as I know, has been able to justify itself..." ***(MOH 1913)***

Successive reports routinely presented details of cancer deaths in Leicester by age, sex, incidence and type. This gradually began to throw some light on the physical nature of the disease and its possible cause.

It was reported in 1921 that there were 307 cancer deaths, of which 23 (8%) were of persons under 40 years of age, 114 (37%) aged between 40 and 60, and 170 (55%) over 60 years. These figures suggest that cancer is a disease of late-middle/old age rather than just old age. However, figures five years later show a shift towards the over 60 years group with 60% of deaths, and a slight fall in the proportion in the 40 to 60 group (32%). Unfortunately later figures used different age bands although the basic pattern remains the same. Thus in 1934, 55% of deaths were in the 65 and over age group and 37% between 45 and 64 years of age. By 1948 the proportion of the older age group had fallen to 50%, with a increase in the 45 - 64 group (42%), but the reason for this is not immediately evident.

The most interesting figures relate to changes in male and female deaths. Prior to the First World War, cancer was seen to be primarily a female disease and the health statistics bore this out. Thus in both 1901 and 1911 almost two thirds of cancer deaths were amongst women. However in 1909 a shift towards increased male cancer was already being noticed:

"...It is of interest to note that the increase in cancer deaths which is taking place throughout the country has been almost confined during the last few years to cancer deaths in males. Some years ago the increase occurred chiefly amongst females..." ***(MOH 1909)***

By 1921 the balance had shifted quite dramatically to a rough balance between the sexes which, apart from an odd temporary shift in 1934, continued through to 1950.

Explanation for the earlier predominance of female cancer deaths was related largely to the incidence of cancer by type/location:

"...One other fact in connection with this disease is worthy of mention, and that is that females are much more subject to it than males. We invariably find more women dying from it than men, and the difference is very much greater than can be accounted for by the greater number of women in the population. The explanation lies in the fact that the sexual organs in women in the population are specially liable to be attacked by the disease..." ***(MOH 1909)***

It was recognised over the entire period that the main incidence of female cancer was of the breast and uterus. In 1921 these together

LEICESTER CANCER COMMITTEE.

CANCER OF THE BREAST.

ADVICE TO WOMEN.

"This leaflet is issued by the Leicester Cancer Committee because so many women die from Cancer of the Breast whose lives might be saved if the advice here offered were promptly acted upon.

"The Leicester Cancer Committee has been formed at the suggestion of the Ministry of Health, and consists of representatives of the Health Committee of the Corporation, of the Royal Infirmary, and of other public bodies, together with a number of representative medical men.

"Of all forms of cancer, Cancer of the Breast is one in which, if it is treated in an early stage, there is a good hope of getting rid of the disease.

"In laboratories and hospitals all over the world workers are trying to discover how to prevent and how to cure Cancer. At present there is only one method known to us which offers a reasonable hope of complete cure, viz., removal of the growth by operation.

"Cancer begins as a localised disease, i.e., it is confined to the part of the body where it starts.

"Therefore, **if discovered early enough,** Cancer of the Breast can be entirely removed, and there is then comparatively little risk of its reappearing or recurring.

"Everything thus depends :—

(a) Upon discovering the disease in the earliest stage;
(b) Upon having an operation performed at once.

"Unfortunately, Cancer of the Breast at the outset often causes no pain or inconvenience. It appears merely as a little lump or thickening in the breast. It is easy to think that this little lump, which is not at all tender or painful, is nothing to worry about.

"Moreover, no one likes the idea of a surgical operation, even though (thanks to anaesthetics) this is painless, and though (in the case we are considering) the operation involves practically no danger to life.

"Many women, therefore, after they have discovered a lump in the breast, put off going to a doctor until it has grown larger and has perhaps begun to get painful, and the most hopeful time for operation may then have slipped away.

REMEMBER ! — DELAY IN THE CASE OF CANCER IS DISASTROUS.

"It is true that Cancer may sometimes return after an operation has been performed, and it is these cases of recurrence which make many people think that all operations for cancer are useless; yet if they knew the truth they would understand that it is **the delay before operation** which is almost invariably to blame.

"The Leicester Cancer Committee, therefore, earnestly urges every woman who discovers a lump or thickening in her breast, to **consult a doctor at once,** and if he advises an operation, to follow his advice.

"These remarks about the danger of delay in Cancer of the Breast also apply to this disease in other parts of the body, both in men and women.

"In conclusion, there is no reason to think that Cancer is either infectious or contagious.

Honorary Secretary,
Leicester Cancer Committee.

Notice issued in 1924

accounted for over 42% of such deaths. In 1948, of the 257 female cancer deaths, 96 (37%) were still related to these two causes despite increases in other forms of the disease.

Amongst males the main forms of cancer tended to be liver, stomach and gall bladder, although the 1921 report notes 15 deaths from cancer of the mouth, tongue and pharynx - the latter two possibly related to the old habit of tobacco chewing.

Discussions of the causes of cancer were inconclusive and reflected the continuing bafflement of the medical authorities. Some causes put forward were better explanations of heart disease. The link between cancer and older age was pursued but eventually seen as not providing a sufficient explanation.

There continued to be considerable discussion of possible causal links between cancer and diet:

"...There are many who believe that in some way the diet of modern civilised races is connected with the causation of cancer, and that too rich a diet, especially one too rich in animal food, is to blame. Certainly there is a great contrast between the comparatively simple dietary of primitive peoples and the varied, complex, and highly elaborated dietary of civilised peoples today. It is also argued that the amount of meat flesh food consumed per head has enormously increased...

"...Others believe that constipation - which is so common in modern civilised life - and the chronic toxaemia of poisoning of the system by certain waste products which accompanies it - is an important factor, especially as regards cancer of the bowel.

"This theory is not really inconsistent with the previous one as constipation is largely dependent on the dietary and habit of life... Unfortunately none of these theories as to the causation of cancer are altogether satisfactory, nor apparently will they fit the facts." **(MOH 1923)**

Dr Millard was not convinced of a link between cancer and diet nor between cancer and constipation. At an early stage in the debate he had raised the idea of life-style and the modern way of life as possible factors:

"We have no reliable knowledge as to the real cause of cancer, or why it has so greatly increased, though there are reasons for believing that it is in some way a symptom of modern civilisation. The most highly civilised people appear to suffer much more than comparatively uncivilised and primitive races leading a simpler life." **(MOH 1916)**

"...There is no doubt that in modern civilised life, especially in these days of motor transport, very many people eat far too much in proportion to the exercise they take or the physical work they have to perform, and this is especially true, I believe, as regards the amounts of animal food consumed..." **(MOH 1923)**

The most poignant statement on the cause of cancer was made by Dr MacDonald in his Report in 1950:

"Recent research has shown that there is a definite association between cancer of the lung and smoking. This has been proven statistically. Cave canem!!" **(MOH 1950)**

It is interesting to see how such discussions

looked at causal factors but they lacked the necessary research and they remained unresolved. Yet by the 1970's some of these factors were accepted and were now properly explained following research.

The only comforting early discovery was that cancer was not an infectious disease in the normal sense of it being passed on from person to person:

"...There appears to be no reliable evidence that doctors or nurses ever catch the disease from their patients, or that even those living in the closest possible association with persons dying from cancer, e.g. husbands, or wives of the patient, are any more liable to the disease than other people.

"This is something to be very thankful for, not only as regards the healthy, but also as regards the sick; the lot of the latter is often bad enough as it is, but if their friends and relations amongst whom they live were to regard them as a source of danger and treated them as lepers, their lot would be infinitely harder." ***(MOH 1932)***

Meanwhile, what could be done for victims of cancer given the then state of knowledge? All agreed that early diagnosis was important but recognised that many people were reluctant to visit a doctor until any help was ineffective. Public notices were issued by the Medical Officer and the Corporation encouraging early diagnosis.

There was however no effective cure:

"As regards remedial measures once the disease has supervened, many lines of treatment have been advocated, but it may safely be said that the treatment offering the best hope of escape at the present time is early removal by the surgeon's knife wherever, owing to the situation disease, this course is practicable. Radium appears capable of curing some superficial forms of cancer but usually can only cause amelioration..." ***(MOH 1913)***

Little had changed by 1950. X-rays had advanced diagnosis and radium treatment had improved, but chemotherapy and radiotherapy and the more sophisticated surgical techniques and drugs were still a long way away.

Heart disease

This covers a range of conditions, although most people tend to group them together. There is *'ischaemic heart disease'* strongly related to diet (e.g. fatty foods), smoking etc., and *'cerebro-vascular disease'* (that is a 'stroke'). There are common elements between them - high blood pressure and life-style. There is a third and separate rare form related to infant mortality - blue baby syndrome, a congenital heart disease.

Heart diseases were not notifiable and we therefore only have the numbers of deaths. Over the period from 1900 to 1950, deaths more than trebled from 304 to 948. Between 1900 and 1935 the number of deaths rose steadily, if slightly erratically, with an inexplicable peak when they rose from 322 to 520 between 1910 and 1911 only to immediately fall back the following year.

From 1934 to 1937 deaths rose by over 80% from 417 to 771, to reach 847 in 1940. There are no figures available for the next three war years but evidence suggests a temporary respite. Deaths then rose again from 1944 to 1947 at the previous rate. There is no immediate explanation for the dramatic rise from 1934 - other than to surmise that the dramatic reduction in death from many of the diseases of childhood, adolescence

Groby Road Hospital, Cardiac Ward

and adulthood was allowing people to 'enjoy' those of older age. It may also be linked to changes in lifestyle and diet which have been regarded as significant factors in the development of both heart diseases and cancer.

The incidence of heart disease by age group increasingly shifted towards old age. Thus in 1935, 65% of deaths were in the post 65 year group and 26% in the 45 - 64 group. By 1948 the figures were 76% and 19% respectively.

In terms of male-female incidence, there was a continued tendency towards more deaths amongst women - for example in 1948, 53% female to 47% male deaths although the proportion in the post 65 year age group is 57% and 43% respectively. No clear explanation can be given, it may be related to earlier deaths of men from other diseases and the increasing proportion of women living into old age.

In spite of the relentless growth of heart disease there was no discussion of it in any of the Medical Officer's reports for the entire fifty year period. There was one small reference in the 1942 Health Report when it was noted that heart and vascular deaths accounted for 38% of all deaths in Leicester - the largest single cause of death.

Were the Medical Officers distracted by issues which they deemed to be of greater public concern? Was heart disease an accepted 'normal' fact of life and especially of old age and for which little could be done? There were other diseases which fell into this category of 'normal' which attracted greater attention.

Tuberculosis

Tuberculosis is not a disease of the natural environment; it is a social disease of civilisation.

There are contrasting historical views of it. There is the romantic one of the pale, delicate, languishing young woman beloved by her suitor but soon to be separated by death, Mimi in *La Boheme* being the classic operatic model. The male version is the young creative genius doomed to die young and here the model is the poet Keats.

The real view is of adolescents and younger adults struck down in their prime, a product of densely populated cities. Poor housing, over-crowded living space, crowded and ill-ventilated factories with noxious processes, poverty and poor nutrition produced a self perpetuating cycle of disease. This was the situation in Leicester in 1900, a legacy of late 19th century urban and industrial growth:

"This disease is the cause of so much economic loss to the Nation, and of so much domestic sorrow and loss to the family, attacking its victims as it does during the active working years of life, that no other disease approaches it in importance. As, moreover, phthisis must be regarded as largely a preventable disease, it is only fitting that it should be considered at some length..." ***(MOH 1908)***

Tuberculosis or *phthisis* or *consumption* is the result of an infection caused by a bacillus known as the tubercle bacillus, *Mycobacterium tuberculosis*. It affects various parts of the body, but is predominantly a disease of the lungs (*pulmonary tuberculosis*), which destroys the lungs. The most common form is spread through the air, through the frequent coughing of a sufferer and the spread of copious phlegm, but also dried phlegm on floors and in dirt. Whether a person exposed to the bacillus catches the disease depends upon the strength of his or her immune system, but in poor environmental and nutritional conditions this is likely to break down. The nature and conditions of the disease were long known in medical history.

In Leicester there were lengthy discussions going back to 1851. The figures for TB deaths show the scale of the problem. In 1900 Leicester was still in the midst of the massive increase in TB inherited from the last years of the previous century. There were 210 deaths in that year. By 1905 it had reached its highest peak of 353, a 68% rise. It was not until 1930 that it dropped temporarily to the 1900 level. The figures began to fall back and level out between 1907 and 1911, but there was a further peak in 1917 (342 deaths) followed by a welcome fall over the next three years. They rose again but from 1926 there was a more consistent fall in deaths with sudden short increases - 1933 (268 deaths), 1947 (188 deaths) and in 1950 (25 deaths). The disease was one of the major killers accounting for 10% of all deaths in 1910 and still over 8% in 1930.

The peaks during the two wars were in part a consequence of the poor conditions and nutrition resulting from the wars. The persistently high figures during the late 1920's and early 1930's were perhaps due to the effects of the Depression.

With such a terrible history, it is not surprising that the Medical Officer of Health and other medical authorities discussed the possible causes of TB in Leicester at length.

Early reports focused upon factory conditions. Concern was frequently expressed about the general conditions in Leicester's factories, notably in the many workshops with cramped conditions and poor ventilation. The reports began to look at the incidence of TB amongst particular occupational groups. For example, the 1901 report showed that of all total TB deaths (273) the largest single occupational group were tailors (33 deaths, i.e. 12%). Attention was drawn to the footwear trade where there were 52 deaths (19%) and to one particular process- 'finishing', where there were 21 deaths:

"...one is struck by the large number of 'finishers' in the shoe trade who succumbed to Phthisis. A shoe manufacturer in the Borough to whom I submitted the figures, informs me that the figure is unduly high having consideration to the relative number of hands engaged at 'finishing'. If this is so, it would seem that the 'finishing' process is an injurious one, and this is only what might be expected when the dusty nature of the process is remembered... I have also visited and inspected a number of other trades and manufacturing processes carried on in the Borough, but with one or two minor exceptions, I have not seen anything specially calculated to be prejudicial to health..."
(MOH 1901)

"Some trades and occupations suffer much more from consumption than others, the worst being those in which dust of a metallic, irritating nature is liable to be inhaled e.g. steel grinding. It has long been known that shoe-making is one of the bad trades as regards this disease, though the reason for this is not definitely known. Coal-mining, strange to say, is one of the good trades."
(MOH 1905)

Considerable efforts were made, mainly through notices in factories, to make employers and employees aware of poor ventilation as a cause of TB. After 1910, interest in the workplace declined as many old workshops were replaced by modern factories with improved ventilation and by new process methods. Another consideration may have been the effects of Factory Acts. Nevertheless, it would be a mistake to assume that this cause had been eradicated.

The debate turned to issues related to social, family and housing conditions. These were seen eventually as the prime source of the disease.

TB was always regarded as a disease of later adolescence and early adulthood, that is *'the prime of life'*. In 1901 deaths by age-group across both sexes shows that the greatest incidence was amongst the 20 - 30, 30 - 40 and, to a lesser extent, the 40 - 50 age groups (29%, 22% and 18% respectively) whereas only 9% of deaths were in the 10 - 20 age group.

Evidence suggests a more complex pattern with striking differences between men and women. A report by the Medical Officer in 1901 showed that of the 273 TB deaths 162 (60%) were amongst men. There are considerable differences within these figures for men and women. For men, 7% of deaths were amongst boys under 10, only 5% of deaths were in adolescence (10 - 20 age group), and an even distribution amongst the main working age-groups: 20 - 30, (26%), 30 - 40 (25%) and 40 - 50 (21%). By contrast, 11% of deaths amongst women were girls under 10, 15% in the adolescent group (10 - 20), but over 32% in the 20 - 30 group, a surprisingly high figure, and only a modest proportion (18%) in the 30 - 40 group.

Can we offer some reasons for these differences? The male figures may be strongly related to occupations - men tended to dominate the trades noted above, as well as jobs with high physical toil, but this does not explain the low figure amongst adolescent men. The high figure for the female 20 - 30 age-group and possibly the adolescent group may arise from a combination of the burden of child-bearing and rearing and the demands of work, given the importance of female workers in Leicester's traditional industries. Related to this may be *'self induced malnutrition'* on the part of women in these groups who went without food in order to feed husband and children.

Contrary to the prevailing idea, the figures above also show that the incidence of TB amongst younger children (under the age of ten) was quite substantial. Concern was expressed over this, and especially the problem of 'pre-tubercular' children:

"The so-called 'pre-tubercular' children ranged from about 6 to 14 years of age - all were ailing and unable to attend school - many had not been to school for months. In a number of cases there was a family history of consumption, either a parent or brother or sister having died of the disease. Many of the children had chronic coughs and were puny and emaciated. In most of the cases the home conditions were unsatisfactory, either from poverty, lack of proper attention, or other causes..." ***(MOH 1911)***

[Copy of Notice.]

THE IMPORTANCE OF FRESH AIR.

Over 250 persons DIE FROM CONSUMPTION in Leicester every year.

PERSONS WORKING IN FACTORIES are liable to suffer from Consumption to a much greater extent than those whose occupation is in the open air.

The open-air treatment is the best CURE for Consumption, but PREVENTION IS BETTER THAN CURE, and it is much easier to PREVENT THE DISEASE BY NEVER BREATHING BAD AIR, than it is to CURE it afterwards with fresh air.

All employees in factories are urged for their own sakes to INSIST ON HAVING THE WINDOWS AND VENTILATORS OPEN, if only a little.

Never mind a slight draught. It is better to have too much fresh air than too little.

One person objecting to having windows or ventilators open may be the cause of a great number of other persons being SLOWLY POISONED BY BAD AIR.

If obliged to close ventilators during bad weather, do not forget to open them again when the weather improves.

REMEMBER, persons working in a close, vitiated atmosphere often fail to notice how bad the air has become.

EMPLOYERS are particularly advised to see that all windows and ventilators are set wide open during meal times. This is most important.

Issued by the Sanitary Committee,

Sanitary Office, Town Hall, Leicester. *Medical Officer of Health.*

Notice issued for display in workshops and factories, 1905

There was particular interest in family relationships and TB, and especially the extent to which hereditary as opposed to inter-personal infection was a factor. There seemed to be little support for a pure genetic hereditary link, although there was a belief in the idea of 'hereditary disposition'. The Chief Medical Officer in his report in 1904, having given details of a survey of family history in 176 TB cases in Leicester, concluded:

"...In other words, in over 60 per cent of the cases there was a history of other members of the family or household having already been attacked by this fell disease! How far these figures should be taken as an inherited tendency to consumption is a debated point. The more modern view is that very

many, if not most, of the cases should be regarded as having occurred through direct infection from one person to another living in the same house. Evidence is accumulating to support this view but there is no doubt that a constitutional weakness or similar tendency to consumption often is inherited, though actual infection afterwards is necessary before the disease can develop." ***(MOH 1904)***

In the same report the view moves to the probable link between inherited tendencies and living conditions:

"...The peculiarities transmitted from parent to offspring have been brought about by the mode of living adopted by the parent or their ancestors. These inherited physical tendencies can doubtless be much modified by environment or manner of life. In fact, the whole question of the prevention of consumption is largely bound up with the great social problem of poverty." ***(MOH 1904)***

The significance of the living conditions and poverty is shown by the following sequence:

"Mr L dies at home from consumption. Is nursed by his wife, who at the time appears to be well and fairly strong. Both wife and baby, a few months old, sleep in same bed as Mr L. Considerable carelessness in disposal of sputum etc. Wife's brother came to live at the house for a time, and he then slept with Mr L. There was stated to be no history of Consumption in wife's family. Sequel: the wife, the child and wife's brother all contracted the disease, and two of them have since died." ***(MOH 1902)***

Eventually it was recognised that the fundamental causes of TB were poverty, poor overcrowded housing and poor nutrition in which personal infection was a consequence rather than a cause. The so-called hereditary predisposition was in fact an inability to break the cycle of TB being passed from parents to children who then infected their children.

As the causes and nature of TB became better understood attention turned to the issues of combating it. There was little the public health authorities could do to overcome fundamental environmental causes of over-crowding and poor housing; this came later in the 1930's with slum clearance and public housing. Little could be done directly on poverty, although a lot of preventative work could be done through existing public health work, mainly health and welfare provision but also education and an awareness of healthy living. The other area of action was through hospital and post-hospital provision.

An important initial requirement was the notification of TB to give a clearer measure of the problem. This would enable the authorities to secure the early diagnosis through doctors rather than the sufferers. Notification was introduced in 1912. There were problems over the principle of notification and its implementation, especially with some members of the medical profession:

"There are still some practitioners in the Borough who often postpone notifying or informing the patient (or his friend) of the real nature of the disease until it has ceased to be any longer in an early stage. The practice in such cases is to hint at 'weak lungs' and to continue temporising until the physical signs of the disease become quite definite and unmistakable. Unfortunately, this does not usually occur until the disease has made

considerable progress, and it is often quite possible to make a positive diagnosis at a much earlier stage. Especially is this the case when one of the early symptoms is haemorrhage from the lungs… Yet it is not infrequently the case for persons who have had haemorrhage from the lungs to be allowed to return to their usual occupation without being informed of its full significance, or advised to apply for sanatorium treatment …that the hope of effecting a permanent cure may have vanished." ***(MOH 1910)***

"...This leads one to state what is unfortunately only too true, namely, that there are several doctors in town who delay examination for too long, and who, when they do examine make such a hurried and superficial examination of the chest by merely having the clothing loosened about the neck as is so often done. This is of very little more value than applying the stethoscope outside the clothing. Examination of the chest must be thorough and therefore takes time, and often several examinations are required before one can say definitely what the diagnosis is. Sputum examination is of very great importance. A positive result settles the diagnosis, but a negative one does not mean that the patient has not phthisis. In such a case it may be necessary to have several specimens examined before deciding on the diagnosis. Every facility is offered by the Dispensary for examination of sputum and doctors would do well to make full use of this valuable means of arriving at a correct diagnosis...

"...In the past many cases of Consumption have been regarded as bronchitis. Proof of this is seen almost daily at the dispensary, where, on examination of the sputum of a person who states that he suffers from bronchitis, the germs of consumption are found. What really happens, therefore, is that many cases called bronchitis, asthma, or one of the other respiratory diseases, are transferred to their correct groupings, namely tuberculosis..." ***(MOH 1915)***

Eventually notification led to a more realistic measure of the problems of TB. The main key to breaking the cycle of TB was to take the less ill sufferers out of their unhealthy environment into a sanatorium where there was good air, healthy food and medical care. A sanatorium had normally been the prerogative of the rich and not the working classes of Leicester.

The idea of a sanatorium in Leicester was mooted in 1900 but was not to come to fruition until 1914. However, in 1903 an experiment of 'Hospital Isolation of Consumptives' was initiated by adapting one ward block for open-air treatment at the Groby Road Isolation Hospital. From the outset it was stressed that its purpose was *not* curative:

"It should be clearly understood that patients are not admitted with the object of ***curing*** *them, but rather in the hope of benefiting and instructing them - by a practical object lesson - as to the best mode of life for them to adopt. It is hoped that the knowledge thus imparted will extend beyond those actually treated at the hospital. It is hoped, also, that an increased appreciation of* ***the value of fresh air as a preventative****, as well as a curative of Consumption, will be similarly diffused..."* ***(MOH 1903)***

Only patients who had a chance of recovery were admitted and initially for only one month. The regime reflected the stated objective with good wholesome food, fresh air and out-door activities

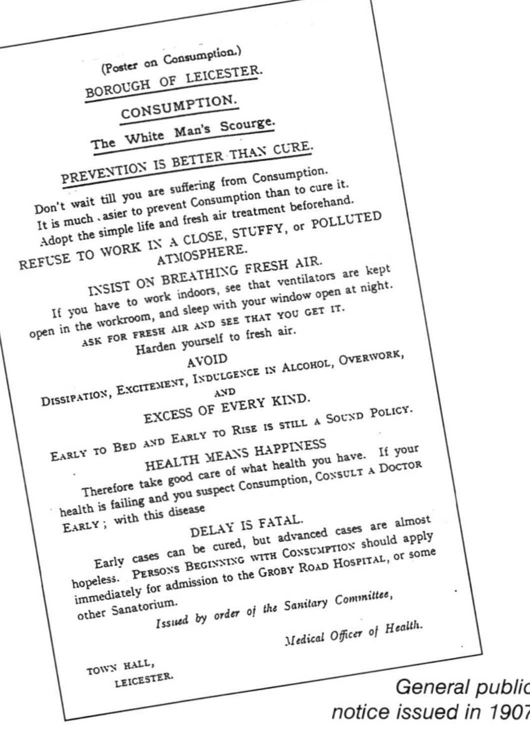
(Poster on Consumption.)

BOROUGH OF LEICESTER.

CONSUMPTION.

The White Man's Scourge.

PREVENTION IS BETTER THAN CURE.

Don't wait till you are suffering from Consumption.
It is much easier to prevent Consumption than to cure it.
Adopt the simple life and fresh air treatment beforehand.

REFUSE TO WORK IN A CLOSE, STUFFY, or POLLUTED ATMOSPHERE.

INSIST ON BREATHING FRESH AIR.

If you have to work indoors, see that ventilators are kept open in the workroom, and sleep with your window open at night. ASK FOR FRESH AIR AND SEE THAT YOU GET IT.

Harden yourself to fresh air.

AVOID

DISSIPATION, EXCITEMENT, INDULGENCE IN ALCOHOL, OVERWORK, AND EXCESS OF EVERY KIND.

EARLY TO BED AND EARLY TO RISE IS STILL A SOUND POLICY.

HEALTH MEANS HAPPINESS

Therefore take good care of what health you have. If your health is failing and you suspect Consumption, CONSULT A DOCTOR EARLY; with this disease

DELAY IS FATAL.

Early cases can be cured, but advanced cases are almost hopeless. PERSONS BEGINNING WITH CONSUMPTION should apply immediately for admission to the GROBY ROAD HOSPITAL, or some other Sanatorium.

Issued by order of the Sanitary Committee,

Medical Officer of Health.

TOWN HALL,
LEICESTER.

General public notice issued in 1907

in summer, along with strict discipline, self-help and later some recreation. Whilst this regime led to a considerable improvement in the overall health of the patients it was unlikely to lead to a permanent cure as patients had to return to their poor environment.

The emphasis began to change in 1914 with the opening of a purpose built Sanatorium next to the Isolation Hospital. There was increasing emphasis upon curative medical treatment and later rehabilitation. The reports over the succeeding years suggested that there was still a somewhat rigid and moralistic style, as though patients were to be blamed for their misfortune.

Medical treatment was based upon the use of tuberculin, an early form of TB vaccination, in a variety of forms recently introduced from the USA. Its use was voluntary and not compulsory - there was still some reservation with regard to its effectiveness:

"I am satisfied that, for the present tuberculin holds the field as the chief, if not the only remedy - tried on a large scale - which can claim in any way to be regarded as a specific. Some patients do well under tuberculin, and appear to derive great benefit even without the advantage of sanatorium treatment; but I do not think, and I never thought, that tuberculin alone would enable us to dispense with sanatorium treatment except in a few cases. The best result, I am satisfied, is to be combining both lines of treatment..." ***(MOH 1913)***

In the mid 1920's other therapies were considered or used experimentally. One drastic treatment involved the use of *'sanocrysia'*, a combination of salt of gold and sodium aurithiosulphate. Any improvement in the patients using this was attributed to being in the Sanatorium and not the treatment. Another and far more successful development in the mid 1930's was *'Collapse therapy'*, involving surgical techniques to collapse and then depress the lung through Phrenic Avulsion or Artificial Pneumothorax. This proved to be successful although in its earlier days it required a long stay in hospital. Combined with new drugs such as streptomycin this became a major form of treatment.

The most important development was purely diagnostic - the use of radiology - this was in use in Leicester in 1912.

The other key development, crucial in the long campaign against TB, was the establishment in 1911 of the Tuberculosis Dispensary. The concept originated in Edinburgh, but Leicester was the first town to establish one. It was funded under the then new National Insurance Act. The Dispensary was located in a converted shop in St. Nicholas Square (now gone) with waiting room, cubicles, consulting rooms and, at an early stage, with X-ray facilities. Later it moved to Grey Friars, then in the 1930's to Regent Road. Initially it was engaged in preventative work and it was successful from the outset:

"The preventative aspect of the work is emphasised, and visits are paid to the homes of cases by both dispensary doctor and nurses to seek out unrecognised cases and, if possible prevent the spread of the disease, but the treatment employed is by means of tuberculin instead of drugs..." ***(MOH 1911)***

The Dispensary worked closely with the Sanatorium and eventually took over most of its out-patient work. It enjoyed good relationships with local practitioners and TB patients or suspected ones were referred both ways. It took on much of the monitoring of TB including details of cases, treatment, etc., and it became increasingly involved with after-care of patients (through the provision of tuberculin). Because of this and its original preventative and monitoring work, it became the campaigning force for improvements in the provision of after-care and rehabilitation, even pressing for better housing.

Both the Sanatorium and the TB Dispensary were undoubtedly instrumental in reducing the numbers of TB cases and deaths in Leicester. By the late 1930's the disease had not been eradicated but its prevalence had declined. There had always been reservations on the part of the authorities at both the Sanatorium and, more vociferously, at the TB Dispensary with regard to their actual collective success in reducing TB. These arose from concern that a patient left hospital with much improved health and returned to home and work, back into the very conditions which had given rise to TB in the first place, undoing all the good medical treatment and care. Such feelings had been advanced earlier:

"...as to the result of sanatorium treatment generally, it is now frankly admitted that, regarded from the point of view of permanency, they do not come up to the expectations at one time confidently held. Probably all that we are justified in claiming is that the majority of patients are temporarily benefited, many of them markedly so." ***(MOH 1920)***

In the case of work, there were concerns with regard to the employability of patients and the problem of their returning to their old trades, where the physical element and the environmental conditions could be detrimental and cause a recurrence of TB:

"...The difficulty such patients experience in obtaining outdoor employment is generally very great, and most of them are therefore obliged to return to their old work in the factory." ***(MOH 1907)***

"...Other regrettable features are that some patients on leaving take up work in the various food trades, as waitresses, dairymen etc., as these specially appeal to the patients as being light or out-door occupations; also in more than a few cases patients somewhat improve, leave the Hospital and subsequently add to their families, which often are

already a burden on the rates or on the State." **(MOH 1916)**

"...another difficult problem is finding suitable work for tubercular patients. One cannot blame employers for hesitating to engage them. Many of them are only fit for light work and cannot be depended upon to turn up with the same regularity as healthy individuals. Light outdoor work, such as would be desirable, is extremely difficult to obtain and is almost always unrenumerative, so for a married man with dependants it is out of the question. Yet we know that in many cases a return to arduous indoor work is simply asking for trouble." **(MOH 1924)**

There were attempts to meet these problems. An initial project was set up in 1907, the outcome of which was not reported:

"...With a view to assisting a few cases to obtain out-door occupation, the After-Care Committee has organised a small Window Cleaning Brigade. This is worked on co-operative lines. The Committee loan to the men a set of ladders and a truck, and the men keep what they earn, subject to a percentage deduction which is pooled to cover working expenses, such as printing, rent of yard where the ladders are kept etc." **(MOH 1907)**

At the Sanatorium schemes established originally to occupy patients whilst in hospital were extended in the early 1930's as a means of rehabilitation, for patients could now stay in the hospital for twelve months. In 1931 there was a 'Patients Work Scheme' involving a variety of crafts - upholstery, basketry, wood-working and even wireless installation, etc. Earlier there had been the development of a Training Colony with 'rural' activities such as pig and poultry rearing, bee-keeping and gardening in the extensive grounds near the hospital - skills not particularly transferable after discharge to a patient living in inner Leicester.

The problems of after-care and living conditions were of particular concern:

"The greatest trouble however, with most ex-sanatorium patients, is the housing problem. Patients after residing for three, six or twelve months under ideal conditions, and in many of whom the disease is practically arrested, have to return to the same conditions which first produced the disease - overcrowded houses in congested areas with totally inadequate ventilation, and into which little or no sunshine can even penetrate. If permanent benefit is to be maintained after sanatorium treatment it is essential for each patient to have a suitable job to return to." **(MOH 1923)**

Below: Groby Road Hospital: Isolation wards (built 1920's)
Right: Aerial view showing entire complex of former isolation and TB wards - nurses home on left, LOROS Hospice centre top

There was little the medical authorities could do to effect changes except to report on the problems - the Medical Officer of Health was very ready to do this. They were encouraged by the beginning of local authority intervention in the housing field:

"We may, however, look forward, I think, to seeing in the tuberculosis death rate some real improvements as the result of the improvement which is taking place in the housing conditions of the people. The large number of subsidy houses which have been erected during the past few years, especially by the Corporation is, I believe, bound to tell in time, for undoubtedly tuberculosis is, to a large extent, a disease of the home." ***(MOH 1927)***

One somewhat modest effort by the medical authorities was the provision of sleeping shelters:

"During the year, with the consent of the Local Government Board, the Corporation purchased twelve wooden sleeping shelters, to be loaned, free of charge, to consumptive patients for use at their homes. There has not been quite so much demand for these shelters as was anticipated. Of course, only a few of the patients who would otherwise be glad of them have the necessary amount of ground. In two cases, this difficulty has

been got over by patients obtaining permission for shelters to be fixed, in one case in a field, and in another in an allotment garden." ***(MOH 1913)***

This arrangement lasted for a few years but probably ended when the shelters needed repair or replacement.

By the late 1930's there was a definite and optimistic view that hospital treatment for all but the hopeless cases followed by after-care had been successful and the disease was declining. The TB Dispensary Report of 1934 noted this:

"It shows that fewer persons each year are being infected and developing the disease. No doubt, in addition to the active measures taken to combat the disease numerous other factors, such as improved environment, with better housing accommodation, better food and clothing, a purer milk supply, less spitting about in public places and so on, are responsible for the reduction. There is now a noticeable improvement in the way in which the public generally respond to advice in regard to Prevention of Diseases." ***(MOH 1934)***

The Second World War temporarily halted this progress and some of these earlier hopes were shattered by the sharp rise in cases and deaths after the war. This was largely a consequence of the war-time conditions and shortages. Shortages of hospital beds meant that sufferers could not be admitted to hospital immediately following diagnosis, thus leaving them in the poor conditions reminiscent of the past and which were thought to have been eradicated:

"...This means that more patients have been nursed at home during the most infectious and dangerous period of their illness, and, with the prevailing overcrowding, this must eventually lead to a higher number of cases of fresh infection due to contact... Another distressing result of this lack of bed accommodation is the plight of the aged and those living alone suffering from the disease and for whom no hospital accommodation is available at short notice. Many of these are shunned by their neighbours because of the infectious nature of their trouble, and when ill, I think it is true to say, many of them are not even properly fed as they are not sufficiently well to join in the scramble for unrationed foods and have to subsist entirely on their rations, often not properly cooked or served. More than one instance has occurred during the past year where, I am confident, neglect and semi-starvation have been material factors contributing to the deaths of patients." ***(MOH 1947)***

This quotation could have been about the situation in 1907 and not 1947. Fortunately these problems were overcome and the numbers of cases and deaths declined quickly. Mass X-ray had started in 1945 but eradication of the disease in this country did not begin until the later 1950's to the 1970's, through vaccination and antibiotics. Progress in the eradication of all such diseases is often fragile, depending not only upon advances in medicine but also upon attitudes and changes in social and welfare provision.

Smallpox and Influenza: Epidemic and Pandemic

The word 'epidemic' arouses fear and foreboding but the hint of 'pandemic' evokes a sense of catastrophe.

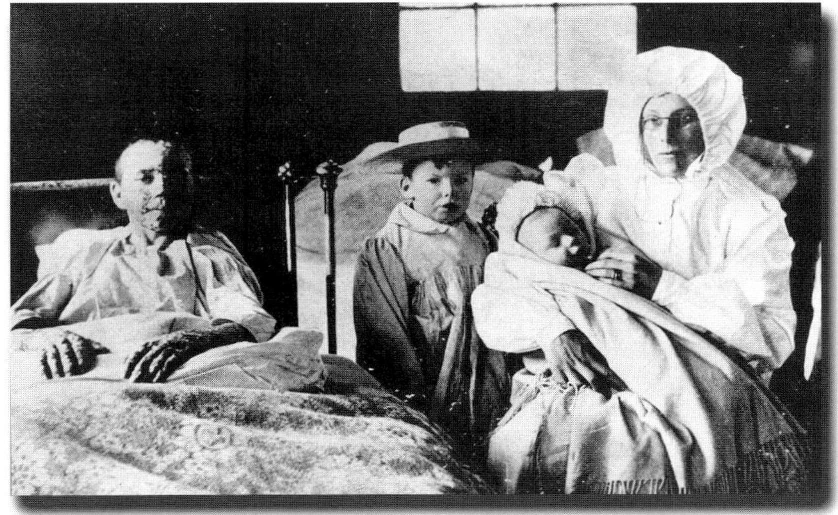

Smallpox epidemic 1903-4: smallpox patient with Dr Killick Millard (right, in gown) and his son (boy with hat) demonstrating a point in the 'debate' over smallpox

An epidemic occurs when a disease suddenly attacks many people in the same region, area, or town at roughly the same time. When an epidemic disease spreads throughout a larger region, continent or the whole world it is called a pandemic. Epidemics were and still are accepted as a fact of life in many parts of the world. Leicester, along with all other British towns, suffered from many epidemics. There was an annual epidemic of summer diarrhoea which affected large numbers of infants and young children, interspersed with frequent epidemics of measles and diphtheria. Epidemics of cholera affected many British towns and created considerable fear and panic.

During the period covered by this book there were two epidemics of local interest - the smallpox epidemics of 1903-4 and the influenza epidemic of 1918-19.

Smallpox epidemics 1903-1904

Historically, smallpox along with cholera ranked as one of the major and most feared diseases and there were frequent epidemics especially in crowded urban areas. Today it has been effectively eliminated across the world. There was never a cure and vaccination was only a preventative measure. The incubation period was relatively long but once the victims were struck down the course of the disease was swift and visual marks of its passage were invariably permanent for the survivors.

Leicester suffered from regular epidemics of smallpox of varying intensity and duration. Prior to 1903 there were major epidemics in 1872 with 346 deaths, and in 1892-3 with 346 cases but only 21 deaths. By comparison there were 406 cases and 21 deaths in 1903, 321 cases but only 4 deaths in 1904. These were relatively small epidemics of *'variola major',* the most severe strain of smallpox. There were further epidemics in 1925 and 1931 but of *'variola minor',* a mild form of the disease which caused few, if any, deaths. The disease then effectively disappeared in Leicester.

The 1903 and 1904 epidemics were considered to be of great significance. The Medical Officer of Health presented special reports on each of them with a full analysis of the progress of the disease, case by case, street by street, with details of vaccination and hospital treatment, etc. This seeming obsession arose from the traditional fear of the disease on the part of the public but also because of a long political controversy over the handling of smallpox in Leicester.

During the 1870's and 80's Leicester had been a major centre for a national anti-vaccination protest. Compulsory vaccination had been introduced in 1853 and reinforced by a further Act in 1861. In 1869 two men were imprisoned in Leicester for refusing to allow their children to be vaccinated. This was the beginning of a long conflict between the authorities and a growing body of protesters, a conflict which became an election issue in Leicester during the 1870's and 80's. This brought divisions within both the Board of Guardians and the Town Council who were responsible for vaccination matters. Compulsory notification had been introduced in 1871 in Leicester but compulsory vaccination and compulsory quarantine were abandoned although the latter was still practised. Out of this had emerged what was known as the *'Leicester Method'* of dealing with the disease:

"The really essential features of the 'Leicester Method' are the prompt notification and isolation of every case of Smallpox, followed by disinfection of houses clothing, etc., and the close surveillance of contacts. Vaccination only enters into the 'Method' to the extent of protecting the staff engaged on Smallpox duty - a most important administrative detail - and as many of the actual contacts as can be persuaded to submit to it." ***(MOH 1903)***

In 1921, a further discussion compared the Leicester Method to more traditional methods:

"A rough and ready analogy may be drawn between the use of vaccination in fighting smallpox and the use of a fire engine in fighting a fire. It may be necessary to turn the hosepipe on adjacent premises, but it would be rather drastic to soak the whole town whenever a fire occurred. Wherever a case of smallpox occurs in Leicester, every effort is made to secure the immediate vaccination of all

who are known to have been in contact with the disease. On average perhaps a dozen people at most require vaccination under this system for each centre of infection." ***(MOH 1921)***

It was not unique to Leicester and the Medical Officers always preferred to call it *'The Modern Method'*.

The 1903 epidemic began towards the end of December 1902, with an initial peak of 50 cases in the middle of January 1903. This was followed by a major peak in the third week of April then, following a brief respite, a further peak in mid May after which the number of cases fell dramatically over the next weeks.

The epidemic started in three places in the town (See Appendix E). On 16 December in the Poor Law Workhouse, a tramp who had walked from Yarmouth carried the disease with him, which was not initially recognised. The patient was moved to hospital on 22 December but six out of 60 inmates had already contracted the disease. From 20 January there were 13 cases in the newer part of the workhouse, mainly women and children, and a final case (male) on 27 January. The outbreak ended. It had been confined to the institution and with a low incidence given that there were 1100 inmates.

The Smallpox Hospital had been immediately re-opened. This was located on Anstey Lane about a quarter of a mile from the new Groby Road Isolation Hospital. It was built of wood and corrugated iron. It had previously been three wards of the former fever hospital on Freake's Ground.

Further cases were from the wider community and there was far greater concern. A young woman living in Coral Street, off Melton Turn, was taken ill on 24 December but her doctor mistakenly diagnosed chickenpox. Twelve days later she visited the Leicester Royal Infirmary as an outpatient; smallpox was diagnosed. With its long incubation period her presence in the crowded outpatient clinic was an important point of contact with other people. Most of the girl's large family caught the disease and there were further cases in nearby streets. One of her sisters attended the Carey Hall Sunday School on Catherine Street and infected six people.

The girl herself was employed at a footwear factory where she worked alongside another young girl who lived in Preston Street, off Humberstone Road. She was the first person to catch smallpox in what was to become the second area of concentration of the disease. This was detected during the first girl's visit to the Infirmary. Several members of the second girl's family contracted the disease as did her next-door neighbour and also a friend living in Great Holme Street. Another case was that of an insurance agent, who caught the disease but was not directly linked to the original two cases although he had a number of clients in Great Holme Street. Thus it can be seen how smallpox spreads.

The epidemic was still at an early stage and during late January, the whole of February and March the number of cases fell away quite dramatically with less than 10 per week being removed to hospital. Suddenly there was a remarkable increase in cases in April and, after a brief lull, a further resurgence in mid May. The Medical Officer of Health described this as *the April "Cloud-burst"*. The first warning involved four unrelated cases on 15 April, rising on the succeeding days to a peak day of 14 cases on 20 April. During the five weeks to 14 May the weekly numbers were 53, 21, 34, 48 and 48, but then they fell to 22. After a further three weeks the epidemic was effectively over. This resurgence was unconnected to the December/January cases and despite the efforts of public health officers only one positive source of the disease was identified amongst 65 cases in the two peak weeks in April.

No particular pattern was discerned. There was a greater number of cases amongst women but this was a mere coincidence. Thirty seven of the cases worked in 32 different work-places, 14 child cases attended 11 schools. The cases occurred in 61 houses across 58 streets and were scattered over a wide area including the northern two-thirds of the town.

No satisfactory explanations could be found. There was an idea that aerial infection from the Smallpox Hospital on Anstey Lane might have been the 'cause' but investigations of wind direction during critical days showed this to be false. In any case, although transfer of the disease is in part through the air, the distance involved is in feet and yards and not miles. The other theory offered was of transmission through unrecognised or undetected cases but the experience of public health officers discounted this.

The 1904 epidemic was of a lesser intensity. It was a relatively weak strain of the disease although there was consternation at having another epidemic so soon after the 1903 one. Were the two linked? Was it in fact one protracted epidemic rather than two separate ones?

By October, the '1903 epidemic' was regarded as being over. There had been no cases in the five weeks from the end of October. The few remaining cases still in hospital had been discharged by 5 December and the Smallpox Hospital had closed.

However, on 9 December three new cases were reported, marking the beginning of another epidemic. There were 14 cases by the end of December, 13 and 26 cases in January and February respectively but 61 in March. There was a surge with 107 cases in April giving a *'cloud burst'* effect similar to the previous year and then the numbers fell away rapidly (52 in May and 33 in June). By August the epidemic was effectively over. Out of 321 notified cases there were only four deaths. One was discounted by the Medical Officer of Health, being the daughter of a tramp who had been in Burton upon Trent where she had caught the disease, two were young children (one of 5 weeks), the only adult who died was reported:

"William B, aged 46, a man of broken-down constitution whose wife had left him on account of his drunken habits..." ***(MOH 1904)***

A feature of this epidemic was its initial link with common lodging houses. Their shifting population presented difficulties in detecting and tracing the course of the disease. This epidemic began next door to a common lodging house in Woodboy Street, off Belgrave Road. The house was occupied by the keeper and he and two of his children caught the disease. It was assumed that his occupation inevitably made him susceptible to such infection. On 22 December a case emerged of a tramp staying at another lodging house nearby in Britannia Street. Then another case of an itinerant knife grinder and his family was found at a lodging house in the same street. There was a case of an itinerant from Nottingham followed by more cases - *'a female tramp, and an Arab person',* who were also in lodging houses. Following these cases, the epidemic became more widespread in the town before reaching its April peak. To the satisfaction of the authorities the incidence of smallpox amongst school children was low, 58 cases of whom only 17 caught it through school contact, a repeat of the experience of 1903. This was significant in light of the vaccination issue.

The epidemic put considerable pressure on the Smallpox Hospital which had only 60 beds and the numbers in need reached over 100. To meet this, the Groby Road Isolation Hospital was emptied of its normal fever patients and closed to such patients for three months, the beds being made available for smallpox sufferers. This was a fully built hospital whereas the Smallpox Hospital had only just been 'erected' and did not have full facilities.

BRITANNIA STREET.
(Belgrave gate.) Wg.

Rollestone & Model LodgingHouses, George Rollestone, proprietor
13 Wilkinson Harry, lodging house proprietor
Court A—
21 Rollestone George, shopkeeper
25 Newton Samuel, shopkeeper
29 Stimpson Mrs. Lucy, shopkeeper & lodging house
Courts C, F & G—
Victoria lodging house, Harry Wilkinson, proprietor
(Cross over
54 Storer Mrs. Elizh. clothes dealer
Court D—
22 DexterGeorgeAlbert, provision dlr
Court H—
6-12 Tomkins Mrs. Ann, lodging house proprietor
4 Weston Matthews, lodging house proprietor

WOODBOY STREET.
(Belgrave gate.) Wg.

1 Cooper William, registered shoeing & general smith
Wilson R. & Co. boot manufacturers
Branch Police & Fire Station, Wm. Hawkins, superintendent
19 Walton Herbt. shopkpr. & grngro
.... Russell square ....
44 Gibbins George, greengrocer & provision dealer & firewood cutter
32 Hallam Mrs. Jane
22 Mason William, boot maker
10 Hill Wm. & Co. provision mers
8 Ellicock Alfd. v. Woodboy Inn
6 & 4 Ward John Henry, shopkpr. & lodging house keeper

Lodging houses in Britannia Street and Woodboy Street which were sources of smallpox, 1904.

There was considerable relief that the attack rates and the mortality rates in Leicester were much better than most comparable towns. Thus the Medical Officer of Health could say:

"On the whole, therefore, Leicester is certainly to be congratulated on having once again escaped lightly. Whether she will always be so fortunate time alone will reveal. To prophesy good is as great as to prophesy evil!" ***(MOH 1904)***

Vaccinations in Leicester had fallen from a peak at the height of the 1872 smallpox epidemic to become virtually negligible from 1888 through to 1903 when numbers rose briefly. During the 1903 and 1904 epidemics there was major concern as to the possible effects of this on the incidence of the disease. Those who had been vaccinated as young children were now old and the majority of the population and especially children were not vaccinated. Hence the detailed analysis of smallpox figures by *old, young, vaccinated, non-vaccinated, re-vaccinated, immune.*

The reports vindicated the Leicester Method but there were still concerns for the future. Some critics, mainly outside Leicester, argued that Leicester as an island of non-vaccination was protected by the large sea of vaccination around it, as most other towns had persisted with the complete vaccination of the population, and full hospital quarantine. The debate re-emerged during the epidemic of minor smallpox in 1925 and 1931 and influenced the debate over diphtheria immunisation from 1934 onwards.

Above: Victoria Model Lodging House, Britannia Street: one of the sources of the smallpox epidemic, 1904
Below: Rollestone & Model Lodging House, Britannia Street: one of the sources of the outbreak of the 1904 smallpox epidemic

Influenza epidemic 1918-1919

The 'flu epidemic of 1918-19 is regarded as the greatest pandemic of the disease, yet the occurrence of such epidemics was quite frequent, the prior one in 1889-91 had caused the death of Henry Tomkin, Leicester's Medical Officer of Health.

Interest in the 1918-19 epidemic lies in part because there are still people alive who can remember it. One eighty-five year old man remembers his mother's death from 'flu in 1918. It was not just the scale of the epidemic but its timing and virulence. The first wave of the illness occurred whilst the Great War was still raging, a situation particularly poignant because 'flu eventually killed more people nationally and world-wide than the war. Contrary to popular belief, the epidemic did not originate in Spain but in the United States and was possibly brought to Europe by American soldiers. This pandemic ranks in world history as equal to that of the Black Death.

The epidemic in Leicester began in the June/July of 1918 when 100 people died from 'flu or the related cause, pneumonia or bronchitis, but this did not cause exceptional concern. It is significant, however, that the overall death rate in 1918 was 18.1 per thousand population, a rate exceeded only three times in the previous twenty years. Coinciding then with the lowest birth rate (14.9 per thousand population), there was a situation where deaths exceeded births for the first time (See Appendix B).

The first *'summer'* wave was followed by the more severe *'autumn'* one from October to December. In the week ending 19 October, 54 people died and the death rate for October and early November was 39.5 per thousand population. It was now recognised that it was a pandemic, in keeping with the national as well as world situation. At its peak 358 people died in the week ending 2 November (this included deaths from bronchitis and pneumonia) with 219, and 156 in the succeeding weeks. Then the epidemic seemed to wane although there were 123 more deaths by the end of December. Over 1000 people died during this wave which was to account for over 60% of the final death toll.

There was a sudden resurgence in mid-February 1919, marking the third and final *'spring'* wave which lasted for about five weeks with about 500 deaths. The final total of deaths from 'flu or bronchitis and pneumonia during the entire epidemic was over 1600 in Leicester.

These figures must be put in perspective. We have the numbers of deaths but we have no numbers of sufferers and therefore no measure of its true incidence. The Local Government Board selected Leicester as part of a national inquiry into the epidemic. It reported in 1920 and estimated that 6% of the population of Leicester caught influenza in the first wave, 14% in the second wave and 8% in the final wave. This gave a total of 30% over the entire period leaving 70% as having escaped. Thirty percent of the population of Leicester was about 65,000 persons. The report emphasised that the epidemic was comparatively short compared with the previous ones, measured in weeks not months and years. Leicester's Medical Officer of Health commented on results of this study:

"The general impression at the time was that a considerably larger proportion of the population were attacked. Impressions, however, are notoriously unreliable. Naturally the numbers attacked would make more impression upon the imagination than the numbers escaping..." ***(MOH 1920)***

There had been an element of panic. Every person would have known someone who had suffered from 'flu or had been related and/or acquainted with someone who had died. Steps were taken to counter such panic - a newspaper report of the Town Council meeting (29 October 1918) records this:

Influenza Epidemic

The Mayor, speaking of the influenza epidemic in the Town Council, said that panic is both uncalled for and inexpedient. It does not do the town as a town any good; it is actually intensifying the epidemic. Psychologists are not certain on the point, but they are inclined to believe that there is a real connection between the 'nerves' and influenza. It may be so. The germ is all around, and fear of catching the disease may actually operate to break down resistance to those germs. The advice of the Borough Medical Officer not to worry is excellent. That, however, does not imply any relaxation of care. To guard against colds, to avoid large indoor gatherings, are elementary precautions which should be observed by everybody. Leicester is faring no worse than many places. Even the countryside does not escape the scourge...

Despite such attempts to quell the panic, the epidemic undoubtedly had a profound effect upon the entire community. The initial shock arose from its suddenness and its virulence compounded by the fact that so little was known about it.

The disease affected all ages and classes of the community. There is no doubt that the greatest incidence of deaths was among those in the prime

INFLUENZA ADVICE.

Official Leaflet.

In islands of the Samoan group having a population of 36,000 there were 7,000 deaths from influenza in a month.

Although influenza masks are advocated for those attending the sick, the Local Government Board does not advise the public to make a general use of them. In a memorandum on the prevention of influenza the Board states that little can be done to prevent any one from falling a victim to the epidemic. No drug has yet been proved to have any specific influence as a preventive, but a standard vaccine used in the Army to mitigate the severity and diminish mortality by raising the resistance of the body has had encouraging results. The danger of staying at work after the first symptoms appear is emphasised as bad for the patient and possibly dangerous to others. It is also pointed out that an infected person talking loudly within four feet of another person may spread the infection in that way. The golden rule is to keep fit and avoid infection as much as possible, cultivate healthy and regular habits, eat good food, and avoid fatigue, chill, and alcoholism.

PREVENTIVE MEASURES.

Colds in the head should not be neglected, and the nose and throat should be disinfected in salt and water. Put a heaped teaspoon of common salt in rather less than a pint of warm water. Gargle the throat with about an [illegible] cupful at a time, and sniff [illegible] the quantity gently up [illegible] able not to go into the [illegible] ly afterwards. Some [illegible] solution of Condy's [illegible] ing.

THE INFLUENZA.

Leicester's Combative Steps.

We understand there has been a serious increase in the number of deaths from influenza in Leicester during the week. Complete figures will not be available until Monday.

At the meeting of the Sanitary Committee, yesterday, after hearing the report of the Medical Officer of Health (Dr. C. K. Millard) on the situation, it was decided to enforce the Public Health (Influenza) Restrictions Act, 1918, which provides that no place of entertainment must run for more than four hours without an interval of at least thirty minutes, during which the building is thoroughly ventilated. This will, of course, affect several of the picture theatres of the town.

The Watch Committee have stopped the children's benefit performance at their picture theatres, and have excluded all children under 14 from all ordinary performances at those places. Posters have been issued urging the public to avoid crowded gatherings of all kinds, and insisting upon the importance, in the event of anyone sickening with the disease, staying at home and going to bed. There is no doubt the disease is largely spread by persons who go about after they have sickened. This is a dangerous thing to do and thoughtless towards others.

The Education Committee have closed a number of schools. There is a great need at the present moment of nursing assistance, both in the town and at the Isolation Hospitals. As regards the home the assistance is largely needed at night, and the services of anyone willing to sit up at night in order to relieve friends who are getting worn out would be greatly welcomed. Such assistance [illegible] voluntary or otherwise.

Leicester Mercury, February 1919

of life - 40% were in the 15 - 35 age band and 23% in the 35 - 60 group. The rest were split between the children under 15 (24%) and the elderly (14%).

The proportion male and female was 40% male to 60% female. Of greater significance is that amongst women 66% were in the combined 15 - 35 and 35 - 60 age groups. The 315 female deaths in the 15 - 35 group accounted for 27% of all 'flu deaths. An initial explanation is that these would be predominantly mothers/wives looking after husbands/children; with many husbands being away in the war, it would be just children. A consequence of this was that many soldiers returned from the war as young widowers, often with young children! The incidence of such deaths would inevitably be a factor in the demographic changes in Leicester in the 1920's and 30's (See Appendix B and C).

'Flu was not a disease of the poor, as with some diseases, for it affected all social classes and all parts of the town. Whole families were hit and often parents and children had the illness at the same time.

The pattern of 'normal' life in the town had already been disrupted by the war and the 'flu epidemic brought other problems. Schools (and Sunday Schools) were closed for extensive periods and by the end of October, during the peak wave, school attendances were below two-thirds and many teachers were absent. Business and industry likewise was disorganised which aggravated their existing difficulties due to the war.

It struck at the public and medical services who were responsible for dealing with the epidemic. As it was a national epidemic no help from outside the area was available. Once the severity of the epidemic was recognised there was a meeting between the Sanitary Committee and various representatives of the medical professions and organisations. All normal non-emergency work in the Public Health and the School Medical Services was suspended; this enabled medical officers, doctors and nurses to be allocated to influenza cases. TB patients, scarlet fever and convalescent patients in the Isolation Hospital were, where possible, sent home which released 70 beds for 'flu cases. The beds were allocated to households with extreme problems, particularly where the entire family was ill. The Medical Officer's report noted a household with one member already dead and an unsubstantiated source reported that a household was discovered with four dead members. The death rate of 'flu cases admitted to hospital tended to be high. There were difficulties in transporting so many patients and the Fire Brigade allowed the use of their motor ambulances.

In homes where there was a particularly high incidence of 'flu, their families and friends found themselves unable to cope with the constant pressure of caring for the sick, especially at night. To meet this, unsuccessful attempts were made by the public health officers to attract volunteers. Agencies such as the District Nursing Association made themselves available for this and other work.

'Flu sufferers, or more likely their dependants, sought some help from their doctor but many more went to the chemist shops. A report in the Leicester Mercury in 1994 (more than 75 years after the epidemic), emphasises the enduring nature of memories of these experiences:

Fighting the flu epidemic

My item recounting a Glenfield reader's childhood recollections of the 1918 Spanish flu epidemic in Leicester brought memories of that time for Mrs Bettina Tunnicliffe.

In a small way she helped her father, a chemist in Waterloo Street, Leicester, play a part in fighting the epidemic.

"My mother helped in the shop when assistants had the flu and she took me with her", explains Mrs Tunnicliffe who was then five-years old.

"Every evening a queue stretched from the chemist's shop almost down to London Road Railway Station. The medicine on prescription was free but patients had to take their own bottle or pay a penny for one. Father filled the bottles with a reddish brown mixture which he made up in bulk, called Mist Expectorant. Mother stuck the labels on the bottles and I handed them out."

She recalls she often fell asleep in the dispensary as her parents worked up to 10 p.m. or until there was no medicine left. "We didn't get Spanish flu and I've never had flu in my life."

There were distressing and macabre problems at the peak of the epidemic related to the disposal of the dead. One firm of undertakers had 11 funerals booked for one Monday morning and a wreath maker supplied nearly 150 wreaths in one week. There was a particular problem of physically disposing of the dead. Undertakers already short of staff due to the war could not cope, especially in making coffins. Initially the Corporation made some employees available but eventually the Tramways Department offered help and assembled about 100 coffins at cost in its workshops. A further problem was of removing bodies to the cemeteries and mortuaries; to meet this the Health Department used an ambulance from the local branch of the Red Cross Society.

The memories of the epidemic are not just of its scale and virulence but of an overwhelming sense of helplessness. Despite influenza's long history little was known of its cause or nature, and therefore of a possible cure or amelioration of its worst effects. Only in 1930 was real progress made in understanding the nature of influenza but, because of its particular characteristics, it continues to present problems.

What did you take if you got 'flu in 1918-19? There were no anti-antibiotics and although aspirin had been developed it was not readily available in this country. There would have been a reliance upon older prescribed medicines as well as home-based ones, some of doubtful efficacy. Some of these contained laudanum and alcohol. During the final stage of the epidemic in Leicester questions were raised concerning *'the inadequacy of whiskey'* in the hospital. The *'Mist Expectorant'* referred to previously was for the resultant cough rather than the 'flu itself. The epidemic provided opportunities for the marketing of a range of patent medicines and appliances and opportunistic applications of products not normally related to the illness. A household compendium gave the following advice:

*"**Influenza (Treatment):** Keep in bed, if fever is present give aperient No. 4. In early stage give a hot bath and afterwards a hot drink, and see that the bed is well warmed. Antifebrin in ten-grain doses may be given during the fever. With weak pulse give brandy. Lung complications should receive their appropriate treatment. In convalescence, a nutritious diet, fresh air, and take No. 27 as a tonic"*

No. 4 was a laxative! *"James's powder, five grains; calomel, three grains: in fevers, for adults. For children, the following: powdered camphor one scruple; calomel and powered scammony, of each nine grains; James's powder, six grains; mix and divide into six powders. Half of one powder twice a day for an infant a year old; a whole powder for two years; and for four years, the same three times a day."* No. 27 was *"Disulphate of quina, half a drachm; dilute sulphuric acid, ten drops; compound infusion of roses, eight ounces; two tablespoonfuls every four hours, and as a tonic in the stage of weakness succeeding fever."*

It is interesting to note that the basic treatment today has not changed regarding rest and warmth. The medicines may have changed though suggested remedies such as Venos and Beechams Powders still exist, but the brandy might not be prescribed nowadays!

Typical adverts 1880-1919

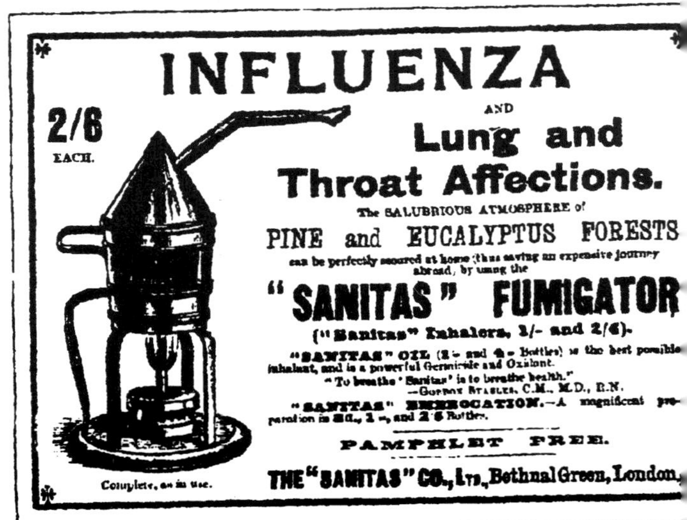

ortifies the System against

NFLUENZA INFECTION.

communication received from a Doctor:—

"A cupful of OXO two or three times a day will prove of immense service as a protective measure. Its invigorating and nourishing properties are most rapidly absorbed into the blood, and thus the system is reinforced to resist the attacks of the malady. It will be apparent that a strong, healthy person will escape contagion when the ill-nourished one will fall a victim, consequently, one's aim must be the maintenance of strength."

The benefit to the community of a concentrated Fluid Beef OXO is greater than ever in the present day; it increases nutri and maintains vitality in the system, and thus an effective resist is established against the attacks of the influenza organism.

OXO appreciably compensates for the shortage of meat.

Sole Proprietors and Manufacturers: OXO Limited, Thames House, London, E.C.4

FIVE HUNDRED THOUSAND DIE

Every year from LUNG DISEASE, which in too many cases is the result of a NEGLECTED COUGH OR COLD. To prevent this, every house in Great Britain should have a supply of WAND'S COUGH CURE ready for use at all times.

RELIEF IN FIVE MINUTES!

The rapid, most certain, and speedy cure for Coughs, Colds, and every disorder of the Throat, Chest, and Lungs proceeding from Cold.

WAND'S

RESTORATIVE TONIC

COUGH CURE

Cures Nineteen out of Twenty!

THE GREAT SUCCESS OF THE DAY!

SALE RAPIDLY INCREASING.

SEE TESTIMONIALS & OPINIONS OF PRESS WITH EACH BOTTLE.

"Worth Five Pounds a dose,—it cured me after the doctors gave me up."
"Thirty Years' Cough Cured by one bottle."
"Consumptive Coughs, Spitting of Blood, Night Sweats, cured by one bottle."
"Several years of Throat Irritation cured by one bottle."
"Severe Bronchial Cough and Difficult Breathing cured by one bottle."

Numerous Coughs and Colds cured by third dose.

It is pleasant to the taste. Children like it. Try it, and in a short time the most violent Cough will be removed.

Sole Proprietor—STEPHEN WAND, Chemist, Haymarket, Leicester.

In Bottles 13½d., 2/9, and 4/6. A great saving in the Large Bottles.

The most Singular and Valuable Discovery ever made!

WATSON'S

COMPOUND CASTOR OIL PILLS

THE BEST MEDICINE KNOWN.

A safe and speedy cure for Indigestion, Biliousness, Headache, Dizziness, Wind, Flatulency, Costiveness, Piles, Disordered Liver, and all Complaints of the Stomach and Bowels; they Purify the Blood and renovate the whole system.

Prepared only by the Sole Proprietor, S. WAND, Leicester. As heretofore by JAMES WATSON. And sold retail by most respectable Medicine Vendors throughout the kingdom.

Price 7½d., 1s. 1½d., and 2s. 9d. per Box, or per post for Stamps.

A considerable saving is effected by purchasing the larger boxes.

Groby Road Sanatorium: TB Ward with veranda, 1935-6

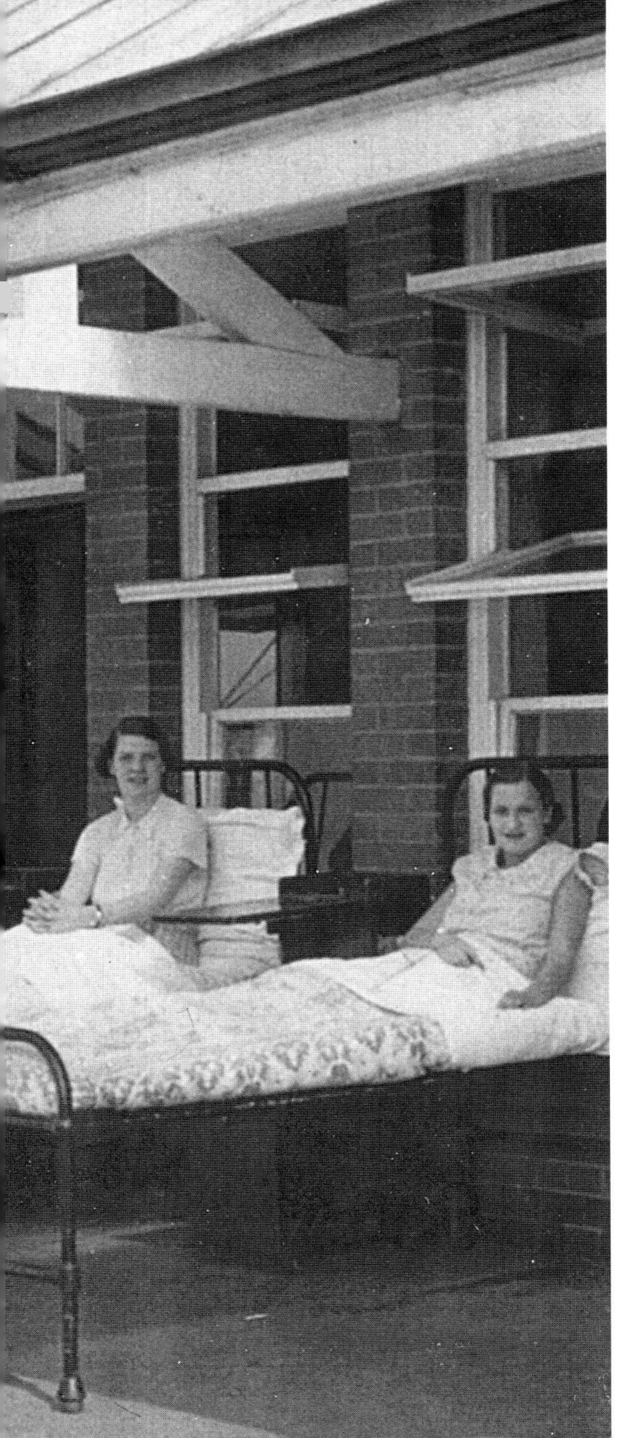

Part Two

Getting better, being cared for

What happened if you were ill? What was the provision of hospitals, clinics and doctors?

If you were old and destitute and could not look after yourself, or you were young and abandoned and in need of care - where did you go? What sort of organisations ran the various hospitals and institutions? Were they charities or some sort of voluntary organisation? Were they run by a public authority such as the Town Council or the Poor Law Guardians? Did you have to pay for medical and other care? How did you find the means to pay for it? Was any of it free? If not, what did you do? What was available to you and your family depended entirely upon your social and financial circumstances.

The next sections look at these aspects of health provision as experienced by the patient or recipient and by the carers.

North Evington Poor Law Infirmary (temporarily the NE War Hospital): Ward 14 with soldier patients, c.1916

Health Provision

You fall ill! Where do you go? There is relatively little information on the provision of doctors in Leicester during this period. Most information was gathered from local directories. In 1904 in Leicester there were about 105 general practitioners. A crude calculation means that there was one doctor for every 2106 people. By 1938 the number of doctors (153) and the population had grown to an average of one doctor for every 1770. In 1951 there were 163 doctors.

The average number of patients per doctor masks considerable differences between doctors' practices before the NHS. Some doctors in Leicester had fewer but more wealthy patients, whilst in the poorer areas doctors had a higher number of patients. In 1945 in a practice in Glenfield/Anstey the local doctor had 5000 patients.

In 1904 about two-fifths of practices were located in the upper middle/middle class parts of the town and about a quarter in the lower middle class areas. There were some around the town centre but this included the fashionable parts such as New Walk and not just the poor parts. There were very few doctors in the heart of the really poor areas. It should be noted that many doctors saw patients at the dispensaries of the Leicester Provident Dispensary or the People's Dispensary or in their own homes.

There were only 19 dentists in Leicester in 1904, yet by 1938 there were 86. Poorer people visited a dentist only if in great pain as you had to pay. Schoolchildren could go to the school clinic. There were few opticians but you could buy a pair of spectacles in Woolworths.

In 1904 there were 58 chemists/druggists shops distributed throughout the town. These were mainly single or two branch shops. T. E. Butler, Son and Company, a local firm, had 13 branches, being one of the first multiple branch chemists. The other well known local firm of Wands had six shops. Many people got their medicines at the dispensaries of the Leicester Provident Dispensary or the People's Dispensary. Many doctors had their own dispensary. In addition there were 17 herbalists and 15 'drug dealers'. By 1938 there were 96 retail chemists which included branches of Boots, now a major national firm, Wands still existed and there was Youngs the Chemists and Jacobs. In 1951 there were still only 96 retail chemists listed.

The provision of hospitals and related institutions was confusing in terms of who ran them, how they were financed and the sort of care they provided. Except for the Poor Law Guardians, many of the institutions were a mixture of charities and voluntary bodies, being a legacy of the past. The local authority had a relatively small role. During our period there was a massive expansion of medical provision in actual building and in the range of services, and most of this was undertaken by the local authority. On the eve of the NHS it had become the main provider of health care, and the role of the charities, etc. had diminished both relatively and absolutely. (See diagram in Appendix F)

In 1900 the Leicester Infirmary was the only hospital which offered a reasonable range of medical treatment. It consisted of three separately financed hospitals - the Infirmary itself, the Children's Hospital and the obsolete Fever Hospital. The hospital was founded in 1771 and was a charity. This meant that its capital and income were raised through major donations, gifts and legacies, from private individuals, but also the Saturday Hospital Society, a voluntary organisation, was already one of its main sources of finance. In 1902 over one-third of the Infirmary's income of £12,158 0s $4\frac{1}{2}$d came from the Society. In 1938 it provided two-thirds of its income and in 1945 about a half. The war-time Emergency Medical Service provided the other half. There were fewer and fewer rich donors and flag days were just not enough!

The hospital until the middle of the 19th century was on the southern edge of Leicester with fields beyond it. By 1900 it was tightly surrounded by mostly working-class housing in a triangle of land marked by Infirmary Road, New Bridge Street and Knighton Street. The houses along Knighton Street and Parliament Street were acquired and later cleared and built upon. There had been major expansion on the site in the 1880's by the conversion of existing buildings, and there was the reconstruction of the Children's Hospital in 1914. There were other developments in the 1920's and 30's, mainly renovation and extensions to existing buildings. The need for nurses' living accommodation was partly met by use of properties in Aylestone Road and University Road. Thus the Infirmary was a maze of buildings of various ages and many of these can still be seen, dwarfed by the maternity unit and the large ward blocks of the 1980s and '90s.

Matching the building growth were significant developments in the range of medical facilities offered. In 1902 the Infirmary had 244 beds. During that year it dealt with 2884 in-patients, 20,956 out-patients and 396 children. The average cost of each in-patient per week was £1 4s $3\frac{1}{2}$d, and for out-patients 2s $4\frac{1}{2}$d. In 1939 there were 622 beds used by 9372 in-patients, by 1945 the number had reached 13,028. The biggest growth was in out-patients, reaching a peak of 29,093 new cases in 1943 (excluding casualty patients), although numbers in both cases had fallen by 1945.

Until the late 1930's any convalescent facilities were provided by the Saturday Hospital Society. In 1937 the Infirmary opened the Zachary Merton convalescent home.

The Infirmary was strictly a general hospital but there was a limited range of medical conditions it would treat. There was a lack of facilities for fever diseases. To meet this, the Town Council had built a Fever Hospital on Freake's Ground in 1875 - located on the high ground above Fosse Road North, behind the present day Stephenson Drive. The wards were constructed of wood and corrugated iron, originally as a temporary measure. The only remains today are rough ground behind the gatehouse on Fosse Lane.

The Medical Officer of Health argued the case for a new Fever Hospital:

"...there is a necessity for such a Hospital, wherein to isolate not only Scarlet Fever, but also Typhoid, Diphtheria, and other infectious diseases (other than Small Pox), no one will gainsay, the only wonder is that the Council as a body has not risen

to the occasion long ago, and provided Leicester with an Infectious Hospital worthy of such an important Town, and a Town that in other municipal and sanitary matters generally takes the lead."
(MOH 1894)

The Council did *'rise to the occasion'* and purchased a large piece of land outside the town boundary. It included the site of the Groby Road Hospital (now closed), and Gilroes Cemetery. It stretched from Groby Road across to Anstey Lane and was chosen for its healthy position:

"Having a nice slope towards the south, the buildings will be able to be so placed so as to get all the available sunshine into them, a most important factor in Hospital construction."
(MOH 1896)

The hospital was opened in 1900. The Fever Hospital on Freake's Ground was closed, but in 1901 three wards were taken down and rebuilt on the Anstey Lane side of the Isolation Hospital as a smallpox hospital, which was to be needed in the 1903-04 smallpox epidemics. Later, when not required for smallpox, it was used as a Children's Hospital, particularly for TB, and then exclusively for children from 1938 despite its dilapidation.

The healthy aspect of the site of the Isolation Hospital made it the preferred choice for a Sanatorium for the treatment of TB:

"...The splendid situation of the Groby Road Hospital on the borders of the Charnwood Forest built as it is on a gentle slope, facing south, with pleasant grounds and surrounded by delightful country, admirably fits it for the open-air treatment of Consumption. Indeed, the institution might

Groby Road Hospital: original main administration building of Isolation Hospital (built 1899)

almost have been built for this purpose, for each block possesses its own covered verandas facing south and west. The necessary staff already exists, and would not need to be greatly increased..."
(MOH 1901)

In 1903 one block at the hospital was experimentally used for TB cases. Its success led to a purpose built sanatorium opened in 1914 next to the Isolation Hospital and jointly administered with the Smallpox Hospital. The extensive land allowed not only for future expansion (there was no major building until 1937 when the nurses home was opened) but also for farming, horticultural and related activities for the TB patients.

The Sanitary Committee had for some years been concerned about the provision of maternity and infant care. Many innovations had been made in the field of maternity and ante-natal clinics, the Milk Depot and the training and employment of midwives and health visitors, some in conjunction with voluntary organisations.

Hillcrest Hospital: formerly Swain Street Institution (the Workhouse) built 1836

Prior to the First World War there was limited maternity hospital provision for working class mothers and most births took place in the home with the help of handywomen and with private and later municipal midwives or doctors, if you could afford them. The Leicester Royal Infirmary was not a maternity hospital. There was the Bond Street Maternity Hospital, the only dedicated maternity hospital, run by the Leicester Provident Dispensary, and the North Evington Poor Law Infirmary, both opened in 1905. These together provided about twenty nine lying-in beds. The number of beds was later increased at Bond Street and a dedicated maternity unit was built at the Poor Law Infirmary. However, there was a need for further provision and in 1919 the Sanitary Committee purchased Westcotes Grange, a large mansion standing in its own grounds located on Westcotes Drive. There were a number of private maternity homes around the town, but these tended to be exclusively for middle-class patients.

There was one other institution which provided hospital care but for most people it was one to be dreaded and avoided. This was the Workhouse. Known as the 'Swain Street Institution', it was a Victorian edifice built in 1836 and located on the high ground on the edge of Highfields above the Midland Railway Station. This had hospital facilities but also accommodated the old, destitute and itinerants. A hospital for the poor sick, the North Evington Poor Law Infirmary, located at the top of Gwendolen Road, was opened in 1905.

The Poor Law system was abolished in 1929 and replaced by the Public Assistance Board. The hospital at North Evington was taken over by the Leicester Corporation and became a general hospital - the City General Hospital. This led to controversy over the needs of the destitute sick - no longer accepted at the City General. The Swain Street Institution, renamed Hillcrest Hospital, now run jointly by the Corporation and the Public Assistance Board, became a hospital for old destitute sick, but still had the workhouse for other destitute people and itinerants. In 1948 Hillcrest came under the control of the local authority and the hospital under the Health Authority. Despite such changes its 'workhouse' image remained until its closure in 1977, and its eventual demolition took place with no regrets by many older residents of Leicester.

The Poor Law Guardians were also responsible for children in need, orphans and children of

City General Hospital: exterior of original ward blocks built c. late 1900's/1920's

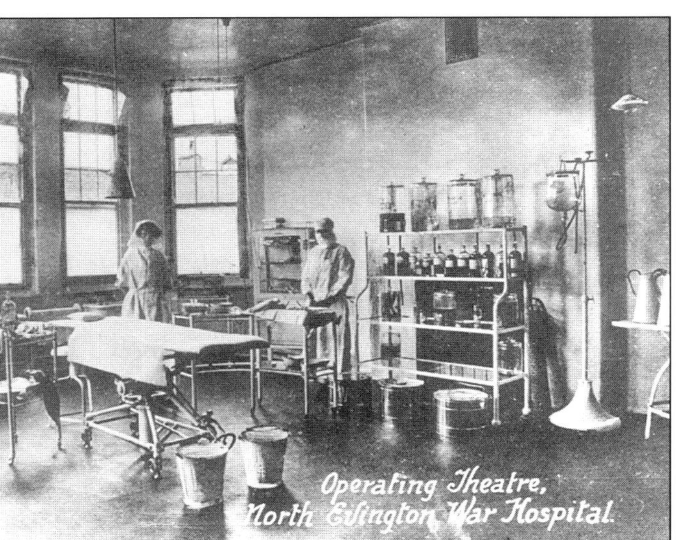

North Evington Poor Law Infirmary (temporarily the NE War Hospital) Operating Theatre, c.1916

City General Hospital: aerial view, c.1930

Countesthorpe Cottage Homes: general view (sports field in the fore-ground was part of the farm)
Right: Foundation stone, 1884

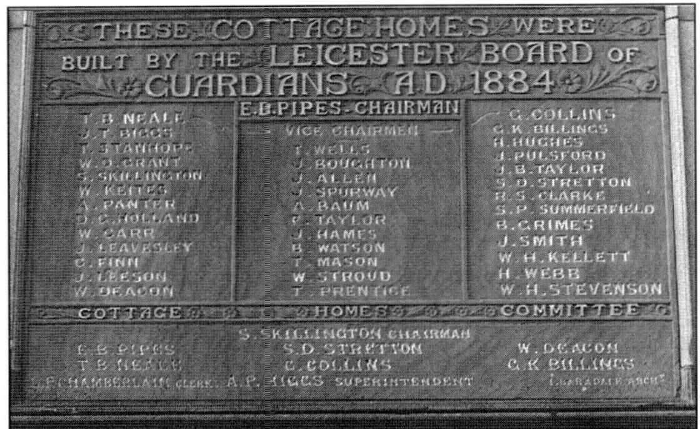

destitute families. Originally they were accommodated at the Swain Street Institution but this was seen to be unsuitable, so in 1894 the Cottage Homes were built in the country on the west side of Countesthorpe. After the abolition of the Poor Law, the Homes came under the Corporation to be administered by the Countesthorpe Cottage Homes Committee, a part of the Education Committee and, after 1948, by the Children's Department.

In the 1950's attempts were made to change the Victorian legacy of the Homes as the policies and practice in child care were changing. By the 1970's most of the houses were empty and boarded up. The houses themselves have been sold off to private individuals and to a housing association.

Reference has been made to the Saturday Hospital Fund which was correctly called 'The Leicester and County Saturday Hospital Society'. This was a working class self-help organisation founded in 1903 as a result of a meeting convened by the Leicester District Trades Council:

"...for the purpose of submitting proposals that there should be an organised effort by the workers to increase the annual income of the Leicester Infirmary, and provide the necessary funds for the establishment of a Convalescent Home... It was thus that upon that eventful evening the meeting pledged full support and a scheme was born - The Leicester and County Saturday Hospital Society." ***(Extract from 'Leicester and County Convalescent Homes Society; Sixty years caring for the convalescent' on its Diamond Jubilee, 1963)***

The subscriptions were initially established:

"Those earning 10s a week and over shall pay one penny per week, and all those drawing less than 10s one halfpenny a week to the fund."

It was a success. Money was collected through the co-operation of local firms who collected monies by deducting the subscription from the pay of the contributing workers. The title 'Saturday' almost certainly refers to the fact that Saturday was the normal pay day for most people working a 5½ or 6 day week:

"their co-operation in granting facilities to permit contributions to be deducted from pay where their employees expressed a willingness to join the fund."

By the end of the first year 236 firms involving 32,500 workers contributed £5129, and 70% went to the Leicester Royal Infirmary and the rest was retained for the establishment and maintenance of a Convalescent Home.

The subscriptions were revised over the years. In 1938, given the rising costs of treatment, they were raised to 3d per week (yielding £50,000). In 1939 the contributions amounted to over £80,000. 1945 was probably the peak year with £97,000 collected. The introduction of the National Health Service meant that all fund raising and contributions for hospital care were redundant. Subscriptions were reduced to 2d per week for those earning over £2 per week, and 1d for those earning less. At that time there were still over 2000 collecting centres raising £55,917.

The Society had made a major direct contribution to hospital provision in Leicester and it was also the main provider of convalescent care for ordinary people. The first convalescent home was opened in 1904 at Desford Hall for 50 male patients, followed by the opening of the Swithland Convalescent Home for women in 1912. This was followed by a home for children at 'The Empitts' next to the Swithland Home in 1920. It was replaced later by Roecliffe Manor nearby. Agreements were made with the Infirmary in 1928 and then with the City General Hospital in 1931, giving both hospitals access to convalescent care for subscribing patients.

The 'popularity' of Desford Hall and Swithland Home declined and prompted a change in policy and provision - the aim was to provide convalescent homes at the seaside. The existing homes were eventually handed over to the Leicester Royal Infirmary. In 1932 the Society bought Overstrand Hall in Norfolk. Reciprocal

Leicester Royal Infirmary: copy of poster appealing for financial support, c.1930's

c.1934

PRIVILEGES OF CONTRIBUTORS

Regular weekly contributors to the Leicester & County Saturday Hospital Society are entitled to :—

RECOMMENDATIONS for
LEICESTER ROYAL INFIRMARY

FREE ADMISSION to a Convalescent Home :

Desford Hall for Men
Overstrand Hall (near Cromer) for Women
Roecliffe Manor for Children

TREATMENT for RHEUMATISM
at Buxton or Droitwich.

ASSISTANCE in obtaining
SURGICAL APPLIANCES.

Payment of the Maintenance
Charges at the City General Hospital.

A SUBSCRIBER'S WIFE, AND CHILDREN UNDER 14 YEARS OF AGE, ARE ALSO ENTITLED TO THESE BENEFITS

WHEN ADMISSION TO A CONVALESCENT HOME IS NECESSARY A MEDICAL CERTIFICATE SHOULD BE OBTAINED AND APPLICATION MADE TO—

THE SECRETARY, 3 WELFORD ROAD, LEICESTER.

OVERSTRAND HALL
CONVALESCENT HOME
Nr. CROMER

OPENING CEREMONY

Whit-Monday, 21st May, 1934

Delegates, Subscribers and all interested in the work of the Society are heartily invited to attend the Opening Ceremony of the Overstrand Hall Convalescent Home, on Whit-Monday 21st May, 1934.

THE CEREMONY WILL BE PERFORMED BY
ALDERMAN W. E. HINCKS, O.B.E., J.P.,
THE CHAIRMAN OF THE SOCIETY, AT 1-30 P.M.

Arrangements have been made for a SPECIAL TRAIN from Leicester. FARE 10/- RETURN.

TRAIN TIMINGS

OUTWARD		RETURN	
Leave Leicester -	- 8-35 a.m.	Leave Overstrand	- 6-10 p.m.
" Syston -	- 8-44 a.m.	Arrive Melton Mowbray	9-50 p.m.
" Melton Mowbray	9-15 a.m.	" Syston -	10-24 p.m.
Arrive Overstrand	- 1-0 p.m.	" Leicester -	10-30 p.m.

MEALS will be obtainable on the outward and return journeys at 2/6 each. Early application for meal tickets is essential as the dining accommodation is limited.

TICKETS ALL TICKETS are obtainable ONLY from Messrs. Thos. Cook & Son, Ltd., Gallowtree Gate, LEICESTER; the L.M.S. Railway, SYSTON, and MELTON MOWBRAY.

A Car Park has been arranged near the Hall for the convenience of those going by road.

Above: Overstrand Hall Convalescent Home

Below and left: Opening Ceremony 1934

Roecliffe Manor Convalescent Home for children

agreements were made with a number of other convalescent societies throughout the country, to open their facilities to Leicester patients.

A stay at a Home was free to subscribing members. The Society also arranged transport by train through an arrangement with the railway companies, but this was subsequently replaced by the use of its own coaches.

The Society offered other benefits, some short-lived:

*"**Home Service Help.** Grants up to a maximum of 3/- per day for a period of 210 days, but the maximum payment in any one year will be for a period of 70 days. When a member has received the total of 210 days' payments, no further claim can be made until a total of three years has elapsed."*

One longer lasting development by the Society was the provision of an ambulance service - older readers may remember the distinctive chocolate-brown livery of the vehicles. This service was absorbed into the city ambulance service along with ambulances operated by the St John Ambulance Brigade, following the implementation of the National Health Service.

The Society was restructured and renamed The Leicester and Leicestershire Convalescent Society in 1948. At that time it was thought that there would be no need for its work under the NHS but it continued to run the Overstrand Home. In 1956 it opened a further one at Sheringham Hall, also in Norfolk. Both are now closed.

The Leicester Provident Dispensary pre-dates the Saturday Hospital Society. It was established to provide medical services for working class people in the city and the surrounding areas. It was established by a group of businessmen as a charitable dispensary in 1833 *"for the purpose of affording gratuitous medical relief to the poor, the funds for the support of which were contributed wholly by subscriptions"*. It changed its status to a friendly society in 1862 and was renamed the Leicester and Leicestershire Provident Society, *"the leading principle of which is, that the recipients of its benefits shall contribute towards its support"*. Initially it provided medicine through its dispensary but following its change in status it also provided the services of doctors.

The first dispensary was built at the junction of Causeway Lane and East Bond Street on the site of a row of late 18th century cottages. By 1903 it had 13 branches located around the town. It had a panel of thirty-five doctors, seven midwives and four nurses to serve over 48,000 subscribing members. This accounted for over 100,000 visits and consultations. In 1911 the dispensary work, including the provision of doctors, was taken over by the medical profession to become the 'Leicester Public Medical Service'. The Dispensary retained its other medical services.

More branches were opened over the years. In the late 1930's there were dispensaries in Fayrhurst Road and Winchester Avenue serving the Braunstone and Saffron Lane housing estates, and briefly in Birstall. In 1925 it had sixty doctors on its panel list and dental, ophthalmic and aural services. By the outbreak of the Second World War there were 85 doctors on the panel. The organisation continued until the introduction of the National Health Service when the allocation of doctors and patients became the responsibility of local Practitioners Councils. The dispensary work went to retail dispensing chemists.

Established in 1889 and based in Rutland Street, the People's Dispensary provided an alternative to the Provident Society. In 1904 it had over 8000 members. Admission cost 1 shilling for the initial entrance fee and 1d thereafter for an admission card. It was run by a committee of fifteen including working men but to include three doctors and a pharmacist chosen by subscribers. It had a list of sixteen doctors, one dentist, eighteen chemists and six branches:

"No fines for delays in payment, every subscriber of 5s entitled to a recommendation providing six weeks attendance and medicine."

It was still in operation in 1925 when the entrance fee was still 1s but the admission card was 3d. It was still listed in the local Directory in 1938, although little information was given. For many people in Leicester, the dispensaries were the only access to both doctors and medicines at a reasonable cost.

The Leicester Provident Dispensary also provided hospital care. In 1903 it opened the Provident Dispensary Hospital, later renamed the John Faire Hospital, in Countess Street next to its central dispensary in East Bond Street:

Leicester Provident Dispensary Society: original dispensary and headquarters, subsequently became part of Bond Street Maternity Hospital next door

The John Faire Hospital, Countess Street before closure in about 1950 (incorporated into Bond Street Maternity Hospital)

"to meet the needs of working men and women who are disinclined to accept the charity of the Infirmary, and who cannot afford the charges of nursing home; to meet the needs of those who require the best surgical skill that can be given and the most efficient nursing it is possible to obtain, for a comparatively small payment. The building comprises three wards - two for women and children and one for men. The charges are £2 10s a week." ***(Kelly's Directory, 1925)***

Established in 1905, and better known, was the Bond Street Maternity Hospital. Later officially called 'The Leicester and Leicestershire Maternity Hospital' it was always known to local people as *'Bond Street'*. It was located in seven converted cottages on Causeway Lane, next to the Faire Hospital and the Dispensary. Four were for maternity patients, one or two per room, and the rest were for the training of pupil midwives. In the 1920's a new wing was added to provide fifty beds.

Both the Faire Hospital and the Bond Street Maternity Hospital were voluntary institutions where patients paid modest fees. By the 1940's the Provident Dispensary had financial difficulties and, in spite of help from the City Council, the Leicester Royal Infirmary took over its administration and finance. The John Faire Hospital was merged into the Bond Street Maternity Hospital, which was now a complex of old and relatively 'modern' buildings. It was still a major maternity hospital, alongside the Westcotes Maternity Home and the maternity unit at the City General Hospital. It continued to operate until the 1970's. Such a complex was too old-fashioned and ill-equipped to meet modern needs, despite its cosy and friendly atmosphere. Following a critical report in 1966, it was replaced in 1971 by a Maternity Unit at the Leicester Royal Infirmary with over 180 beds.

There were a number of other private and charitable institutions providing medical or related care, for which there are few consistent records. There were a number of nursing homes and small hospitals located around the city. There was for example, the Highfield Hospital, a charity in Tichborne Street still operating in 1941 but gone by 1951. The Midlands Hydropathic and Sanatorium shown in the 1938 directory was a private hospital at 194 London Road. A hospital providing maternity care was the oddly named, 'Home of Twilight Sleep' in Prebend Street .

The best known and most prominent private hospital was the Fielding Johnson Hospital established in 1925 by Thomas Fielding Johnson, a member of a prominent local business family. This was located in three converted houses on Regent Road. Unusually it provided both nursing and surgical care. It became part of the Royal Infirmary in 1947 and continued to provide private medical care within the NHS until the early 1990's. The attractive facade of the building remains.

There were a number of other charitable institutions, the best known being Wyggeston's Hospital and Trinity Hospital. These were for the aged and still exist. There was also the Leicester Society for the Indigent Old Age, *"established to allow aged persons of good character an annuity of 6d a week and to afford the lady almoners an opportunity of ministering to their temporal and spiritual needs".* The oddly named 'Consanguinitarium' was founded in 1792 by John Johnson, an architect, for his poor relations. It was originally located in Applegate Street but subsequently moved to Earl Howe Street, providing almshouses for five people who received 4s 6d per week. Other almshouses still in existence in 1951 included the Memorial Cottage Almshouses in Knighton Drive, Miss Lawton's Almshouses in Evington Street and the Aged Pilgrims Friends Society's Almshouses in Clarendon Park Road.

Bond Street Maternity Hospital: original cottage buildings 1905, with 1920's extension behind

At the other end of the age range there was and still is the Leicester Poor Boys and Girls Summer Camp and Institute, later better known as the 'Leicester Children's Holiday Home'. This

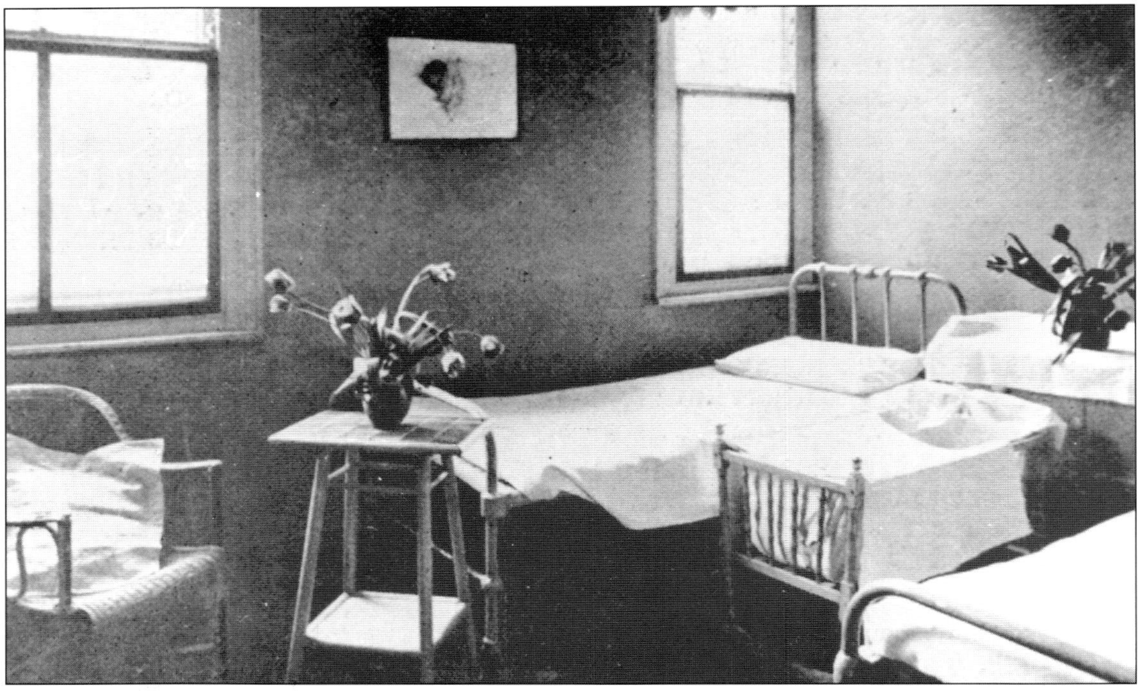

Bond Street Maternity Hospital: two bed room, c.1931

charity was founded in 1898 to provide boys and girls of poor families with a holiday at Mablethorpe. Holidays were spent in tents amidst the sand-dunes, but in 1900 temporary wooden buildings were constructed. By 1919 it was recognised that more suitable and permanent buildings were needed, which were eventually opened in 1935.

There was the Sutton Charity founded in 1853 by the late Benjamin Sutton, for the relief of patients discharged from the Infirmary and the Fever Hospital. In 1902 it had an income of about £840, of which £729 15s, was given out to in-patients, discharged and/or convalescent patients.

Two other areas of medical provision - mental health and the school medical service - must be noted.

In the case of mental care we must initially differentiate between the 'mentally ill' and the 'mentally deficient'. In the earlier years of the century the difference was not always clear, especially when it came to the question of who provided care. Until the late 1860's the Lunacy Commissioners were responsible for the mentally ill in institutions run mainly by charitable bodies, but involving local magistrates and local councils who provided most of the patients. In Leicester, the main asylum was The Leicestershire and Rutland County Lunatic Asylum, dating back to the early 19th century. This was on Victoria Road, now University Road. The asylum took public and private patients from the two county authorities, the Borough and also from elsewhere (patients from Leicester could be sent outside the county). There were complicated arguments with regard to the destitute mentally ill and this involved the Poor Law Guardians. The arrangement between the Asylum and the constituent local authorities was eventually dissolved in 1865 and Leicester built its own asylum primarily for local patients on Gipsy Lane. In the 1930's it was called The Leicester Mental Hospital, and after 1948 by its better known title the Towers Hospital. It still exists. The county asylum was built near Narborough, later to become known as Carlton Hayes Hospital. The 'old' asylum had continued with increased numbers of patients, but it was empty by 1908 and the charity was wound up. During the Great War it was used as a military hospital. The building remains and it became the site of the proposed University College in 1921. Today it forms the administrative buildings of Leicester University.

There was no statutory provision for anyone considered to be 'mentally deficient'. In Leicester there was some provision for those with learning difficulties, and there were one or two voluntary homes. Otherwise, those regarded as *'idiots or imbeciles'* were committed to the asylums or if destitute to the Swain Street Institution. Children who were considered to be more high grade, usually described as *'feeble minded'* and destitute, were admitted to the Workhouse, but could leave when they reached the age of sixteen. For the asylums there was an incentive of 4s a week to accept such patients, an incentive not available to the Poor Law Guardians. This was an unsatisfactory situation and in 1913 new legislation required local authorities to provide residential care. The Corporation opened three hostels but they were insufficient. In 1923 a large house and land at Leicester Frith, beyond Gilroes Cemetery, was purchased for such residential care.

The School Medical Service dealt with various diseases and medical needs in clinics located around the town, some part of schools, some shared with other medical services - Richmond House, Elbow Lane, Clarendon Park - and through the visits of nurses and doctors into schools. It monitored the spread of epidemics and took appropriate measures such as school closure. The Service inspected schools to assess and monitor health standards and general hygiene facilities. They dealt with ventilation, playgrounds, drinking fountains and even the teachers' facilities. They were involved in health education especially over dental care, posture and also issues such as malnutrition.

Most older Leicester-born readers will have memories of the School Medical Service - a nurse

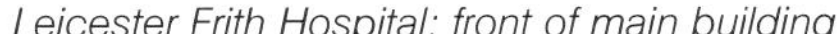
Leicester Frith Hospital: front of main building

Towers Hospital: front of original building, built 1862

checking your hair for 'nits'; inspections for scabies and ringworm; dental appointments at Richmond House; eye tests followed possibly by the issue of wire framed spectacles. The worst that could happen was the school doctor excluding you from school because you or your brothers or sisters had one of the more particularly infectious diseases, or worse one of the contagious diseases - scabies, impetigo, ringworm and even nits - the bright coloured ointments for some of them marking you out. You might however have enjoyed the temporary respite from school.

Until the mid 1930's the School Health Service was separate from the Sanitary Committee, which was to become the Health Committee. The Medical Officer of Health was primarily concerned with the pre-school and post-school health matters and the School Medical Officer was responsible for those of school age. This arrangement worked as there was an excellent personal and professional relationship between Dr Killick Millard, the Medical Officer of Health, and School Medical Officer, Dr Warner. They served the city for over thirty years. When they had both retired in 1935, the Board of Health in London interceded, arguing that the two services should be brought together under one officer. The City Council resisted this and no appointment was made. Later Dr MacDonald was appointed Medical Officer of Health and School Medical Officer, and Dr Turner was appointed as Senior Medical Officer (Education).

The doctor and the chemist

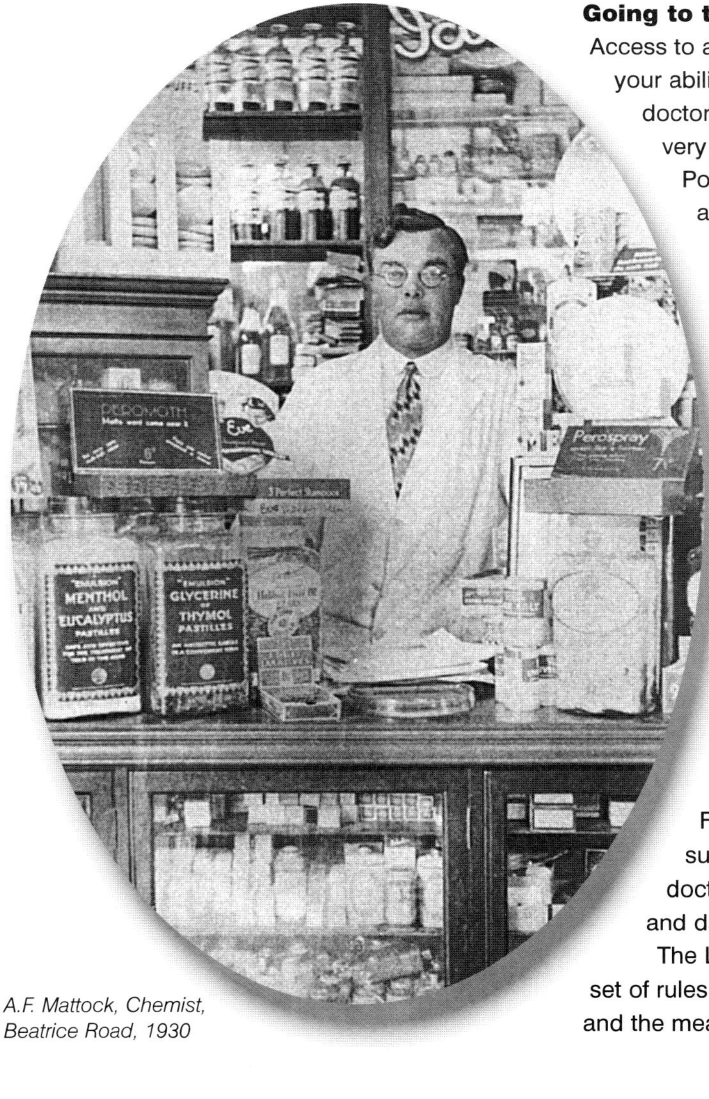

A.F. Mattock, Chemist, Beatrice Road, 1930

Going to the doctor

Access to a doctor was largely determined by your ability to pay. The well-off chose their doctor and paid the necessary fees. The very poor and chronic sick might go to the Poor Law Guardians - the Workhouse and the Poor Law Infirmary. The National Insurance Act of 1911 established the first contributory health scheme for working men. This gave free access to a doctor through what was popularly known as *'the panel'*. The doctor contracted into the scheme was paid a capitation fee for each panel patient. Women, children and the desperately poor were not initially covered.

In Leicester many people would have used the Leicester Provident Dispensary or the People's Dispensary as described in the previous section. Otherwise many joined sickness clubs or Friendly Societies, and paid a weekly subscription. They were run variously by doctors, employers and Friendly Societies and dated back to the previous century.

The Leicester Provident Society had a long set of rules covering every aspect of membership and the means of getting a doctor, medicine and so on.

Membership *"shall consist of servants, working people, their wives and children, who within the opinion of the Board, are unable to pay for Medical advice in the usual manner..."*

To join: *"2. Any such person wishing to become a Member, shall leave his or her name, age, residence, and occupation, at the Dispensary, or one of its Branches, and deposit one month's Subscription, twopence for card and entrance fee of One shilling, in accordance with Rule 3, which will be returned if the Deposition be not admitted a Member...*

"3. Every Member shall pay One Penny per week, but Threepence Half-penny a week shall be the total charge for a man, his wife and all children under fourteen years of age, who will all be entered on the same card of admission. An entrance Fee of One Shilling, and also Twopence per Quarter will be charged on each card towards current expenses... Servants who may be judged eligible by the board, shall pay Five Shillings a year, and not less than half-yearly payments in advance..."

There were separate payments for expectant mothers concerning the midwife's attendance, normally ten days. The fees in full or in instalments were *"One guinea for the first, and Fifteen Shillings for any other confinement..."*, but in some parts of the Leicester area it cost one guinea (21 shillings) for a doctor's attendance and eight shillings and sixpence for a midwife.

There were strict rules for payment of subscriptions with a penny fine for arrears of one month, and after eight weeks you were struck off the lists. It was extremely difficult to be reinstated. Equally strict were the rules for applicants who were already ill: a medical examination was required and the advance payment of subscriptions. For the chronic sick the initial membership was limited to three months.

There were rules and procedures for getting a doctor - home visits, visits to the surgery or visits to a doctor at a Dispensary, including times, etc. Having selected a doctor from the panel list you could only change him/her at specified dates.

There were even rules for obtaining medicines:

"Patients will not be supplied with Medicines in stone or black glass bottles, but must find clear glass white ones; all pills and ointment boxes will be provided by the Institution. Liniments, lotions and all poisonous liquids can only be supplied in blue bottles..."

The overall impression is that the institution was essentially for the relatively healthy, hardworking, thrifty, good living, working person and his family, reflecting the Victorian concepts of 'self-help' which had inspired its founding in the first place.

The private unpublished history of the Glenfield practice by Dr David Parkes-Bowen, who was a partner in the practice from 1951 until his retirement in 1997, gives us some insights into what it was like to be a doctor in the urban/rural fringe of Leicester, rather than in the densely populated town.

The practice was established in 1891 at No. 2 The Green in Anstey by Dr George Harris. However all did not go entirely happily:

"...Dr Wooley who lived on the opposite side of the Green... was already in Anstey, and it seems that the two doctors were not on very friendly terms

because in about 1902 Dr Harris planted some poplar trees to obscure the view of his rival's house. This petty friction between general practitioners was fairly common before the advent of the National Health Service on July 5th 1948, and still occasionally continues to this day..."

At this time, doctors were in competition with each other. The surgery consisted of a small room in the house and patients came through the front door and waited in the hall. He had *'indoor assistants'* who lived in the attics. At a later period there was further 'discord', Dr Filmer Coleman took over the practice from Dr Harris's successor, Dr Williams, in 1938 but:

"...such is the power of the doctor's wife - in those days at least - that Mrs. Coleman took one look at No. 2. The Green and refused to move in. Dr Coleman, therefore, thinking both of domestic harmony and of the increased chances of expansion in a village without a resident doctor, built a new house, surgery and dispensary at 111 Station Road in Glenfield..."

The practice now had two surgeries, No. 2 The Green, Anstey being retained and lived in by a succession of assistants. Some patients at that time had no resident doctor or little choice of doctor in their village and limited access to transport to go elsewhere. It was therefore more convenient for the doctor to go to the patients by setting up branch surgeries:

"...In addition to the two main surgeries there were branch surgeries in Groby at 9 Markfield Road; in Ratby at the first house on the corner of Stamford Street, and latterly in the upper room in the factory on the other corner of the road; and in Kirby Muxloe at 14 Main Street and later in Glenfield at 21 Liberty Road, at a bungalow which has now been demolished. These 'branch surgeries' usually consisted of the partial use of the front parlour of a private house where the doctor and his assistant would sit at the same table - in winter time usually in their overcoats in front of an enormous fire, while the patients waited standing in the cold hall, or even as at Ratby, outside in the street! There were facilities for examination only at the new Glenfield surgery and at Anstey, but of course there were many home visits..."

The majority of patients were 'panel patients' who paid through the contributory schemes already described. Private patients constituted only a small part of the practice.

Most practices consisted only of one or two doctors so the work-loads must have been heavy, including travelling to and from the branch surgeries and the home visits. Surgery hours tended to be short - an hour in the morning and an hour and a half in the early evening. During the war when Dr Coleman was on his own, he served about 5,000 patients but still found time to undertake some clinical work at the Royal Infirmary. Even after the beginning of the National Health Service, Dr Brown, Dr Coleman's successor with newly appointed Dr Parkes-Bowen, (on a salary of £1000 per year and free living accommodation), had 7200 patients across 100 square miles, covering the branch surgeries and patients travelling in from other villages. Eventually these branch surgeries were closed leaving only Station Road, Glenfield which still remains as a practice.

The relationship between doctors and patients

in the period is well described by a doctor in the following extract:

"My family had, like many others, changed little in the fifty years before the NHS started. Whether the incumbent doctor was good or bad made small difference to a patient's future, as most treatment, other than surgery, was powerless to interfere with the course of nature. The good general practitioner diagnosed early those conditions which his surgical colleagues could correct; he was a dab hand with the chloroform or ether; and he wielded the obstetric forceps so that, of good fortune, both mother and baby survived… In the eyes of their patients, doctors have always varied in quality. My grandfather was thought of as autocratic, sound, a good diagnostician, but unbending and distant. Even when I started in my family practice, my father's skills were still remembered, as was his easy charm...

"My uncle… was adored by his older patients but even they realised that he hadn't read a medical book or journal, or attended any form of post-graduate education, since he qualified 40 years earlier. His knowledge of human nature was as extensive as his knowledge of medicine was limited… The practice, like most of those at the start of the NHS, was nothing if not personal: I signed the death certificates for the patients who had been delivered by my grandfather. We knew all 4500 patients by name. We knew the names of their children and their dogs..."

('Bevan's baby', The Times, June 1998)

Getting your medicine!

You could get the prescribed medicine from the doctor himself if he had his own dispensary, or from the Leicester Provident Dispensary or the People's Dispensary. You could go to the local chemist who could also provide you with a range of his own and patent remedies.

You might have gazed around the shop with its ornate coloured glass bottles and secret shelves whilst the pharmacist made up the medicine in a brown, green or clear bottle, or blue if it was really poisonous. The tablets or ointment went into boxes, tins or jars, not the modern tube or capsule.

You would also have noted other products around the shop. He was unlikely to sell the various beauty and personal hygiene products which we see today. Chemists often sold tea - it was deemed to have beneficial effects. There were tonic wines such as *Wincarnis* and *Sanatogen.* There was *Lucozade,* an expensive medicinal glucose drink for the convalescent patient, to be drunk in small amounts. Today it is drunk from a can or bottle like any other sweet fizzy drink. There was a range of both child and adult foods to encourage healthy bodies or to pick-you-up, *Virol, Newmol, Haliborange,* and *Slippery Elm Food.* There was always a set of weighing scales for you and the family, as well as scales with a napkin lined basket on which you weighed the baby. The chemist might have offered dental services on site and ready-made spectacles (which could also be obtained at Woolworths for no more than 6d!).

The chemist may have sold non-medical products such as chemicals and materials for photography and cameras. Two well known Leicester photographic firms Young's and Jessops began life as chemists, selling both medicines and photographic products before concentrating solely on the latter. Jacobs, another local firm still retains an interest in both.

But what sort of medicines were prescribed by

Premises of A.F. Mattock, chemist, on corner of Fosse Road and Beatrice Road in 1930. Business still in existence

Leicester Provident Dispensary Society: former dispensary on Hinckley Road (1867) subsequently a police station, now in retail use

your doctor or sold by the chemist directly to you?

An initial approach is to note what medicines were *not* available. There were none of the antibiotics which dominate modern medicine. The first of what we would regard as an antibiotic - penicillin - was developed in the 1930's, but used only in the very late stages of the Second World War, for the armed forces rather than the civilian population. A nurse working at the City General Hospital recalls using penicillin - at that time by injection and not tablets - for injured soldiers repatriated to Leicester.

Many older people will recall *M and B* tablets, 'named' after the manufacturer May and Baker, as the 'wonder drug'. These were *sulphonamides*. They were developed in the 1930's in Germany and derived from a red dye later named Prontosil. They did not combat the initial infection but infections arising from it. The first ones sometimes had fatal effects but as one retired chemist noted, *"You might almost certainly be going to die from a given ailment, if this new drug overcame it, so much the better!"* Being derived from a red dye they tended to colour a patient's skin red, later white or clear ones overcame this. They were gradually extended and used for a wider range of ailments. Developed in the 1890's, the only 'modern' drug was aspirin which had just come into regular use at the beginning of the 1900s. There were a number of remedies used in hospitals for which specific reference has already been made in previous chapters; tuberculin for TB and antitoxin for diphtheria, for example. There was virtually nothing for many of the common fever type diseases such as scarlet fever and measles.

Many medicines were still based upon traditional materials derived from plants, rather than inorganic materials developed artificially in the laboratory. These included arsenic, digitalis, quinine, strychnine, sodium bicarbonate, sodium bromide and opium. The latter was used extensively well into the 1930's.

About ninety percent of medicines were held in stock and made up by the chemist, either directly from the doctor's prescription or from the chemist's own recipe book. Firms such as Parke-Davis and Welcome already existed and supplied basic prescription materials. There were very few nationally branded proprietary medicines, other than patent medicines, until after the introduction of the National Health Service.

One way of looking at what was prescribed is to look at the old prescription books of one retail chemist, Burfords (later to become W.H. Dennis) in Halford Street. The *'prescription history'* of two customers was extracted from these prescription books for a period of about two years, from which the illness was identified:

Mr A. was a director of a well established Leicester knitwear firm. He lived at a very good address on London Road in Stoneygate. We do not know who his doctor was. He had nineteen prescriptions made up by this chemist between October 1930 and May 1932, he may have had others made up elsewhere as well as purchasing patent medicines. He seems to have been particularly ill during the winter of 1931-32. Over the entire period he had at least six prescriptions for tonic medicines. Tonics of various kinds were regularly prescribed in those days, a practice which most modern doctors would frown upon as being doubtful and unnecessary. These tonics contained a number of ingredients including in Mr A's case strychnine and prussic acid. Did this use of tonics possibly reflect a relatively unhealthy or deficient diet, even in an upper-middle class household such as this? Mr A. also had a number of sedatives both for his heart and his nerves, one of which contained digitalis and another potassium bromide. He also had several medicines for indigestion. Perhaps both of these were a consequence of stress in his work and his lifestyle.

Mrs B. was the wife of a footwear representative living in Clarefield Road, then a new middle class area in Western Park. She had thirteen prescriptions over the same period. She was quite poorly between October 1930 and January 1931 when seven items were prescribed. She also may have purchased patent medicines. Thereafter she was relatively fit. As with Mr A. she had a number of tonics prescribed for her, one again containing strychnine but also one containing cod liver oil, similar to the old proprietary Scots Emulsion. (In the case of one of the tonics, the chemist who advised the author when preparing this section, noted that if he had been the chemist at the time, he would have questioned the prescription with Mrs B's doctor, a Dr M.). Otherwise she had no specific regular complaints but rather a variety of problems - cystitis, several chest and related ailments - one prescription contained tincture of opium and belladonna and she was also prescribed an inhalant, eye ointment (a sty) and for a sore throat quite a powerful medicine was prescribed containing cocaine which was required to be registered as a poison by the chemist. One interesting feature was the prescribing of two or three homeopathic remedies.

The prescription books show the cost charged to both the customers. No medicine cost less than 1s and there were several costing 2s 6d. These were very high prices for that period and more than many working class families could regularly afford. This explains why the dispensary societies and Friendly Societies were so important.

Examination of the prescription books of the same chemist for 1904 showed that the range of medicines had remained largely unchanged over the intervening years.

There was a range of patent medicines available, some of these were prepared and distributed by national firms or local chemists prepared their own such products. A well known local product was Carrs Fever Powders made by a William Carr, a chemist in Wharf Street. There were also Cleaver's cough pills, Martin's baby foods and Morris's liver remedy.

Beecham's Pills were already well established, as well as Venos and Owbridges cough and related remedies - all these products still exist. There were also firms offering a range of herbal remedies. Some claimed to be effective for a broad range of unrelated ailments. There were others which claimed to cure specific ailments including baldness, cancer, gout, headaches, toothache and so on. Besides the well-known ones above, there were 'Harvey's Blood Pills', 'Zam-Buk' - once a well-known skin ointment , 'Gower's Green Pills' (for backache, rheumatism, kidney disorders and numerous other ailments), and even 'Pink Pills for Pale People'. A book entitled 'Secret Remedies', published by the British Medical Association in 1909, suggested that many of the claims were unfounded, that the contents were ineffective and the price high in relation to actual cost.

The retail price of many of them was comparable with those noted above for prescription medicines. In 1909 Beecham's Pills ('*worth a guinea*') cost 1s 1½d for 56 pills (actual cost of ingredients was half a farthing). Venos Lightning Cough Cure was 1s 1½d for a two and three quarter fluid ounce bottle, and Owbridges Lung Tonic was in various sizes, the largest was 6½ fluid ounces costing 2s 9d.

Norman Pilgrim worked briefly in a chemist shop and still has vivid memories of this. He left school in 1935 hoping to become a trained pharmacist, and became an assistant in Peberdy's, a chemist shop on Waterloo Street - now long gone. In the event he did not have the right qualifications and left after a year.

"...I started at work at 12s 6d a week. The hours were 8.30 or 9am to 6pm in the week but until 8pm on a Saturday. These were not bad for shop hours and the boss, Mr Peberdy, came in and opened on Sunday mornings as he lived round the corner in Princess Road. You had to take your own sandwiches but had to eat them quickly, sitting in a corner before the customers all came flooding in from the doctors.

"I had a little counter in the middle of the dispensary where the rough stuff was done, and I had a set of brass scales which I would polish each week. Bob Peberdy, the boss's son, had a little dispensary at the side - a sort of table let into the wall with little bottles, all with their Latin names and just enough to make about one prescription. He had a little balance and one of its pans was just like a watch glass, so you can see how sensitive they were. There was one place I could not go to and that was the poison cupboard. It contained things such as tincture of opium which was still used quite a lot.

"My job was to do what I was told. It might have been cleaning the windows, or scrubbing the floors. Or the boss might say 'these shelves are all sticky', they were covered in saturated solution of sugar. They were 'sticky and horrible' from the necks of the bottles - I would have to take them all down, many of them beautifully coloured, and clean the shelves with soap and water and put

CARR'S FEVER . . POWDERS

BENEFICIAL ALIKE FOR CHILDREN AND ADULTS.

The Best and Safest Medicine for Colds, Feverish Heats, Sore Throats, &c.

SOLD BY ALL DEALERS IN PATENT MEDICINES.

PREPARED ONLY BY

E. CARR, Wharf Street, LEICESTER.

CLEAVER'S COUGH & ASTHMA PILLS.

27 Half-Pence will buy 26 Pills.

Each Pill secures a good night's rest and gives INSTANT RELIEF FOR COUGHS, by dissolving the congealed phlegm, thus producing free expectoration.

Sold in Boxes at 7½d. and 1.1½ by Chemists, or sent post free to any address, on receipt of 8 or 14 stamps, by the Proprietor.

S. CLEAVER & SON, Dispensing Chemists,

Wharf Street and Gladstone Street, LEICESTER.

TIC AND NEURALGIA PILLS (A CERTAIN CURE), 7½d. per Box.

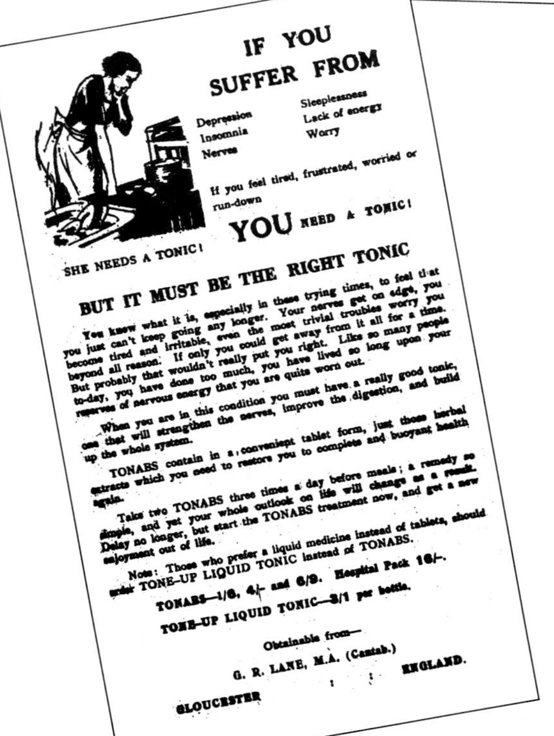

them all neatly back. It was just as likely I would be making up medicines at my counter.

"There were virtually no tablets, apart from aspirin and indigestion remedies. There was a pill making machine but I never ever saw it used. It was nearly all mixtures, ointments and powders. There were very few prepared proprietary prescription medicines - there were things such as glycerine suppositories which were bought in. So the medicines were made up by the pharmacist mostly from his own book. Only later did these become proprietary medicines made by firms such as Parke-Davis, Borrows-Welcome, with their own brand names. We used these firms for drugs and some of their made up products. Otherwise the boss would look at the doctor's prescription and tell me what it was, for example - 'mist sodii sal 12ozs, 1/2ozs' (that is a sodium salicylate mixture, a tablespoonful three times a day). We had a big Winchester quart of it - a large glass bottle with a stopper - already mixed and I would make up the bottle and label it. When we got well down the Winchester we would make a fresh lot. Each bottle of medicine was carefully wiped clean, labelled and then wrapped in a fancy white paper, sealed with red sealing wax and finally labelled again.

"There was Coal Tar Ointment - I had a big mortar, you put in paraffin molle alb - that is white Vaseline - weighed up to the right number of ounces and then I would add coal tar, a blackish-brown syrup, just so much and to smell right, mix it all and then put it into little boxes. I would also make up cough mixtures in the same way.

"We had some lovely mixtures, there were two syrups - glycerphosphate was cherry red and was a pick-me-up like Parish's medical food, and syrup of hypophosphite - a lovely green one which was for nervous disorders and to calm you down. Lots *of people had faith in another calming mixture which had tincture of valerian in it. Powders would not be made up as tablets unless they were bought in as packaged ones. Instead I would make up a large quantity and then roughly divide into small individual quantities which would then be wrapped up into little paper parcels.*

"All medicines contained the basic ingredients made up with water. Sometimes it would say 'menthae' which would mean it was flavoured with mint. It might also have a few drops of chloroform added to the water, shaken very hard (they do not mix very easily) - the sweetish taste of the chloroform took away some of the nastiness of medicine itself.

"Putting a record of the prescription in the book meant that if someone came into the shop saying 'That medicine you gave me last time was really good! Can I have some more?' - so you would then look it up.

"There were patent medicines - such things as Beecham's Powders, which we still have today. There was 'Thermogene' a sort of pink cotton wool steeped in something - you felt that your back was on fire. As for quack remedies - it depends upon what you mean - after all Beecham's Pills were supposed to cure everything, but they didn't. It was not a quack one if people believed that it did them good!

"We got the basic materials from E.H. Butler, and there was Clarke, Nettleships and Bailey, who were in Stamford Street near Cowlings, and we got some things from Richardson's who were then on the corner of Conduit Street and London Road.

We always had a 'wants book'. The boss used to say 'think of the next person, when the bottle is nearly empty, don't wait for it to be empty, put it in the wants book'. He would ring them up each morning, read out the list and they would be round in a couple of hours or so.

"We used to have a home delivery service. Every week I used to take four ounces of neat tincture of opium to a lady who lived in East Street! She must have been in the final stages of cancer or something like that!

"Fielding Johnson Hospital was just round the corner and we did all their dispensing as they did not have their own pharmacy. I had to go there every morning and afternoon to ask them if there were any orders. I would pick up the prescriptions, go back to the shop where they would be made up, and then I would return to the hospital with them later...

"We also provided other services for the customers. We had a large brass syringe that was used for syringing ears. We would remove foreign bodies from the eyes, and splinters from the hands. Also we tested urine - customers would bring in large bottles of urine but for the test we only wanted about half a test-tube. Needless to say, I had the job of disposing of the remainder!

"Besides the usual medicines we sold other products but never photographic products. There were some herbal products. We also made up and sold bottles of shellac mixed with Meths - for household use on furniture or as coatings on electrical wiring."

Another source of remedies were those traditional ones handed down successive generations, or obtained from various household handbooks which contained large sections on illnesses and medical care. One such classic work was *'Enquire Within for Everything'*, which had been published and revised continuously since 1859 and was still available in the 1930's.

Les Gutteridge remembers quite a number of the traditional home remedies:

"Some of them are unbelievable today, my grandchildren look in amazement!... If you got a cold it was nothing for my Dad to give us three drops of turpentine on a spoonful of sugar, that would start you sweating. It did not taste too bad. Mind you it was pure turps in those days!... There was Avroid Ointment, which you got off the market. It was guaranteed to cure anything. I've no idea what it was made of!... There was brimstone and treacle if you had skin diseases or rashes... Besides the sugar and turpentine remedy, for colds, headaches and that sort of thing you got Camomile tea. But say you had 'flu or something like that, you used to have sherry and eggs beaten up - what eventually became a drink - Advocaat. It was a beautiful stimulant to get you back on your feet. Another old remedy for colds and chests was to put some camphorated oil in a towel and inhale. Sometimes if you got a cold, to get you sweating they used to put a hot poker in a glass of Guinness and you got that down, what it did I don't know but this was for the old folks, not for us youngsters!... Then you could buy 'Thermogene' wool, a pink stuff like cotton, if you had got chest problems or bronchitis.

"...There was what you called a wintergreen ointment if you got backache, lumbago or sciatica. But they always said you should wear your mother's old red flannel drawers also for that - they used to cut them up and a sew it on to your shirt tails - often for the old people. Why it had to be red, I don't know... Egg and milk was given especially for diarrhoea. But for constipation they gave you castor oil, so you made sure you did not get that!... I remember I got a rash all over my body - I don't know if it was chicken pox or perhaps eczema, and I had all these sores - the old doctor told mother to wash me down in soft soap, that is pure soap, brown coloured caustic stuff. It was certainly regularly used if you had got chicken pox, as it left you no scabs. I think it was to stop you scratching - it was kill or cure...

"We used bread poultices for boils and abscesses. We also still used dock leaves... I used to get impetigo - I had it every spring and autumn - liquid from the sores would trickle down my face and so make another sore - they used to put a greasy stuff on to stop this and then another white stuff to dry it up, which we got from the clinic down in Taylor Street. I think I was excluded from school. Old folks used to say that when I was seven years old it would go - the strange thing was that when I was seven it did stop although, when I was eighteen, a girl hit me and I got a similar rash around my mouth, and this also lasted for about seven years... For sterilising things we used to buy a red fluid which was in fact potassium permanganate... Of the prescription medicines, I remember that quinine was used quite a lot. There was an iron and quinine mixture - used as a tonic..."

The medical and general household reference books offered remedies for a wide range of ailments and maladies including hysterics, getting rid of freckles and how to 'cure' baldness, which you could make up yourself. '*Enquire Within*' made this easy - you looked up the ailment to find a series of numbers which referred to lists of medicines and ingredients in another section. The range of ingredients was vast, including opium, quinine, sulphate of zinc, carbonate of iron, nitric acid, tartrate of antmony, flowers of sulphur, ergot of rye, syrup of balsam, aloes, muriatic acid, rhubarb, and so on. There seemed to be considerable emphasis upon aperients (i.e. laxatives) - *'In the springtime of the year, the judicious use of aperient medicines is much to be commended' (Enquire Within).* Diuretics and many varied tonics, were widely used irrespective of the initial ailment. Many of the 'prescriptions' read like a witches' brew and would horrify doctors and chemists today.

BEECHAM'S PILLS.

A box of these pills, advertised to be worth a guinea, is sold for 1s. 1½d., and the prime cost of the ingredients of the 56 pills it contains is about half a farthing.

In a circular wrapped round the box it is stated that "these renowned pills are composed entirely of Medicinal Herbs," and cure Constipation, Headache, Dizziness or Swimming in the Head, Wind, Pain, and Spasms at the Stomach, Pains in the Back, Restlessness, Insomnia, Indigestion, Want of Appetite, Fullness after Meals, Vomitings, Sickness of the Stomach, Bilious or Liver Complaints, Sick Headaches, Cold Chills, Flushings of Heat, Lowness of Spirits, and all Nervous Affections, Scurvy and Scorbutic Affections, Pimples and Blotches on the Skin, Bad Legs, Ulcers, Wounds, Maladies of Indiscretion, Kidney and Urinary Disorders, and Menstrual Derangements.

The pills had an average weight of 1¼ grains, and analysis showed them to consist of aloes, ginger, and soap; no other medicinal ingredient was found. The quantities were approximately as follows:

Aloes	....	**0·5 grain.**
Powdered ginger	....	**0·55 „**
Powdered soap	....	**0·18 „**
	In one pill.	

Leicester Infirmary: balcony of Oliver ward and view of other wards, 1910

Life in Hospital

Being sent to hospital meant that you were really ill and there you came into contact with nurses, doctors and surgeons.

Hospital for both patients and carers was a way of life with rules and conventions and divorced from life outside. For most patients, the period spent in hospital was longer than today, longer still if it included convalescent care. It was a highly regulated environment with your days and nights organised for management reasons as much as for medical ones. The only contact with the outside was through limited visiting, perhaps through a newspaper and later through the 'wireless'.

What of the carers? Nurses were all single women and if they married they had to leave nursing. They 'lived in' - in rooms adjacent to the ward or later in a nurse's home on the hospital site or nearby. Their life was highly regulated and controlled in what they were allowed or expected to do - the two usually coincided. The main regulators were the hierarchy of senior nurses headed by the matron.

There were only male doctors to relieve this female dominated world, and they were often superior and aloof. The number of resident doctors was very small in relation to the number of nurses - in the 1930's there were only three doctors, including the Medical Superintendent on the resident staff at the City General Hospital. Their lives were inevitably highly regulated. The people employed on maintenance and other duties were the only other men.

We have no personal accounts of life in hospital for the early period. The reports of the Medical Officer of Health and the Medical Superintendent, and copies of rules and regulations give the odd glimpse of the life and conditions.

Reports over several early years noted the poor and dirty conditions of patients, especially infants and older children. Most notable was the utter malnutrition and lack of stamina giving problems of recovery or even survival. One child of two weighed only 17lbs, but his bed-neighbour of the same age was 32lbs. A neglected boy of 12 weighed 35lbs, though average weight at such an age was 76lbs. The effect of hospital care was remarkable:

"A month's stay in the Hospital has a remarkable effect on some of these poorer children, and one cannot help feeling that a mild attack is by no means an ill-wind to them. On more than one occasion parents have stated that they failed to

recognise their own children, the change not being due to the severity of the illness, but to frequent bathing, adequate air space, and good feeding." ***(MOH 1901)***

Conditions for nurses at the Smallpox Hospital during the epidemic of 1904 were grim:

"...they [the nurses] *were literally steeped in infection. They had to wash and feed the patients; to make their beds and change their soiled linen; to dress their sores and cleanse their mouths (often most offensive in bad cases); to collect and burn the scabs (often in handfuls) that are shed by the patients; and in the event of a fatal issue, to 'lay out' the corpses. Many of them continued on Smallpox duty for many weeks at a stretch without a break. Although the health of the staff on the whole was good, there were times, as might be expected from the arduous nature of their duties and the close confinement, when they would 'run down' and be specially liable, one would think, to contract any infection. At the outset there was no question of their being 'seasoned' to the disease because most of them (prior to 1903) had never seen a case of Smallpox before."* ***(MOH 1904)***

There are a number of accounts of life in hospital from the mid-1930's onwards. One is by a boy who was a patient in Groby Road Isolation Hospital in 1939, when he was nearly 5 years old:

"...I caught diphtheria and was sent to Groby Road Hospital. Young though I was I can still remember the vastness of the hospital ward, for a time I was in a bed near one end of it. I can remember the nurses moving around me. I cannot remember actually feeling ill but yet I have a vague sense of being frightened. I was in hospital for some weeks. My mother, father and sister visited me but could only see me through the windows. The other recollection is having rice pudding cooked with eggs - I still do not particularly like rice pudding! My sister has two particular memories. I returned home with a Cockney accent acquired from a fellow patient and I learnt new words to a well known musical hall song:

Underneath the spreading chestnut tree
Hitler said to Germany
If you want a bedpan don't ask me!
Ask Nurse Casey in Ward Three.

It seems that I adored Nurse Casey!" ***(CH)***

Ron Gurr remembers being in the Royal Infirmary and the City General Hospital for about a year in about 1933 when he was ten years old:-

"...I was out playing in the park and noticed 'bruises' on the front of my legs. When I got home I showed them to my mother and she took me straight to the doctor. The doctor arranged for me to go to the Infirmary to see a specialist. These bumps did not hurt. They were about the size of small eggs on my shins. I saw this specialist and he sent me straight into the Infirmary, I was only ten years old. I was there for about two weeks. They used to bandage my legs along with some calamine lotion and hope for the best! I had a marvellous time. I was completely spoilt as I was in the Men's Ward...

"After about two weeks I was transferred to the Children's Ward at the City General. I was put straight to bed with no pillows and told to keep completely still. Other lads in the ward who could get about would come up to me and I would raise my head. But Nurse Sharpe would shout 'Get your

head down, Gurr!' That upset me, I was not so much frightened as angry! I got a lad to write a letter to my mother for me - she was only able to come up and see me about once a week - saying 'Get me out of here! I don't like it!'. But she didn't...

"I had about six months just lying there. When you are like that you just sleep a lot. I must have been fed. I can't recall anyone sitting me up... Nor can I recall any treatment. I remember this doctor coming round - the bumps had gone down by then - he said 'I want you to tell me if you get any bumps on your arm for that is serious and we must know immediately'. About a week or two later one did appear on my wrist, but every time the doctor came round I would cover it up and never tell him it. I wanted to be out!... They eventually started getting me up. I started off with five minutes, sitting in a chair, which was gradually increased to ten and then fifteen minutes. Then they started me walking. I had to learn to walk again and they did this with a nurse on either side of me...

"During the latter part of the time, there was a sort of reception room at the end of the ward where I used to go for an hour for schooling. A teacher used to come from outside. There was another lad with huge swollen glands. I was getting mischievous by then and I remember knocking the chair away as he was about to sit down. I then felt so horrible about it as it must have hurt him, he cried and the Nurse told me off... I fell in love with the nurses - I thought they were beautiful - except that one - she was tall with sharp features and a sharp nature...

"When I came out I was sent to convalescence on a farm either in Thurmaston or Thurlaston - it was with a family, they lived in a farmhouse, possibly a tied house. I had two to three weeks there and had a wonderful time. They had a shepherd dog and every morning I used to take it out with me and went opening the gates for the horsemen, they sometimes gave me a penny. My mother and aunt used to come at weekends to visit me on the bus - I remember running down the hill to meet them. I think that they paid something like a penny a week [NB. likely to be a Friendly Society]... *I never remember learning what I had got, perhaps they told my mother - my illness seemed to have been some sort of 'rheumatic lumps'. I don't think they really knew what it was."*

The most revealing accounts are those of a group of former nurses, now in their late 70's and early 80's, who trained and worked at the City General Hospital from 1932 until 1948. One worked there until her retirement in 1969.

At the City General you could become a probationary nurse at the age of 18, but entry was 19 at the Royal Infirmary. Nurses were mainly recruited from outside the area served by the hospital - there was no clear reason for this, one nurse thought that it removed any possibility of you knowing a patient. Miss Claye, the formidable matron of the City General in the later 1930's, thought that trainees from the local area would always be going home and so weaken the group identity. One of the few nurses in this group who came from Leicester was accepted only after some questioning of the matron's view by her formidable mother, a local councillor. Many came from economically depressed areas such as Wales and Ireland. The first male trainee was taken on in 1941 as the result of pioneering work by Matron Claye.

Before 1919, training was somewhat rudimentary with many uncertificated nurses. Under the Nurses' Registration Act, nurses were required to be state registered and so the nurses in this group had a systematic training programme and sat examinations. The lectures were normally given by the existing staff sisters and doctors, but by 1937 a tutor had been appointed. Training lasted for three years, four years if you went on to a specialist field such as midwifery.

Trainee nurses spent at least three months on each ward gaining experience in the various specialist areas. At the end of this they took the General Nursing Council's Final State examination for the General Part of the Register. After that they were fully qualified nurses and they now wore a stiff, starched bonnet instead of the 'butterfly cap' of the probationer.

A pay rise awarded in 1918 gave a first year nurse £16 a year and a sister £60. By the 1930s nurses were paid £25 per annum in their first year of training, which in pre-decimal money was about £1 6s 8d per week, with national insurance deducted, rising by increments to £35 in the final year. A sister received £80 - £100. There was no superannuation. In the 1930's they normally worked 11 hours a day for a pittance.

All the former nurses have fond memories of their time there, but are nevertheless quite blunt when describing the conditions, especially for young probationer nurses:

"...It was really slave labour! There was very little domestic help on any of the wards. It was a rigid hard life. Almost military! And worse than that, you were even persecuted by your immediate seniors..." ***(PR)***

The other abiding memory was *"Sister is Sister, Matron is the Law!"*

When Dora Greaves entered nursing in 1932, the hospital had only recently changed from the North Evington Poor Law Infirmary to the City General Hospital:

"I arrived at the City General on New Years Day 1930 in a snow storm. I was met by Sister Phillips, the Home Sister, who showed me to my bedroom and left me to sort my things out. It was a small little box furnished with a bed and dressing table - you stretched across the room and you could touch the walls. There were no curtains and no heating of any description. A paper fan filled the grate of a large open fireplace...

After having supper down stairs with another new recruit, I returned to my bedroom. Hanging behind the door I find a notice 'North Evington Poor Law Infirmary: Rules for Probationary Nurses'. I can't believe it! I check the bed-linen etc. and yes, it was definitely marked 'North Evington Poor Law Infirmary'... I am in the wrong hospital!!! I can remember taking the large stone steps to the ground floor two at a time... Ellen was on duty in the pantry there. She was, unfortunately, completely deaf but she eventually found Sister Phillips who soon reassured me that I was in the City General and that they had not yet got around to changing the labels, etc..." ***(DG)***

You arrived at the hospital and put on your uniform and the soft black ward shoes. You immediately went on to the ward. From the outset it was 'hands on' training. Sister called you *'Nurse';* to the patients you were a nurse, even though you were utterly green and nervous.

The hours were long and the work hard. On the day shift, you were dressed by 6.30am - earlier if it was one of the special days when there were prayers in the chapel at 6.45, then on the ward for

7am. The night nurses would have prepared breakfast before finishing at 8am - they were called back if they had not finished all their duties. You would serve breakfast. The nurses would lay out the table in the middle of the ward with bowl, jug and towels (laid out in a fan) as strictly as a soldier would lay out his kit for inspection. The fires in the wards had to be cleaned out by domestics. Some of the domestics in the 1930's were ex-patients, retained since the Poor Law days, who worked for nothing. One was known as 'Deafie', who was left over from when it was a military hospital. He spent his time following a rota of polishing the ward floors, moving the furniture and beds, and using a heavy concrete bumper covered with a duster.

The nurse would go off for about 30 minutes for a meal break which was neither breakfast nor lunch, *"There were large jugs of sweetened cocoa and rounds of bread (often home-made) spread with dripping, which disappeared like lightning."* She would also tidy her room for the Home Sister to inspect. Back on the ward she would wash the patients and, as there was no running water or sinks on the ward, a portable bath would be filled outside and wheeled in to a bed-side. Soiled linen would be sorted and there was that special job for all probationers - sluicing the bed pans in the 'sluice room'! Junior nurses even dusted the ward. Senior nurses would attend to the medical care of patients - changing bandages and distributing medicine and so on.

"At about 11am screens would be put across the door and Miss Masters [the Matron] *has arrived to do her round. What an elegant lady she is. Tall and slim and immaculately dressed in loose brown gown, the skirt of which only just cleared the floor.*

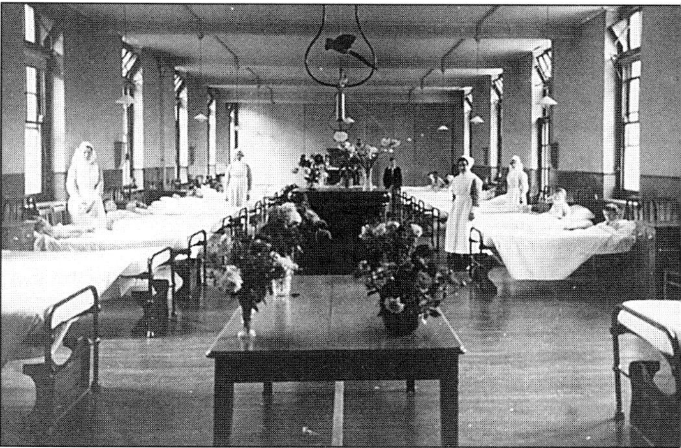

City General Hospital, children's ward 1936 (Ron Gurr is in the second bed on the right)

She wears a large frothy bonnet with strings and bows, and real tatting edges to her collar and cuffs. She seemed to know every patient by name, and needed to know every detail of the various treatments being administered..." **(DG)**

Woebetide the nurse if she did not know the name of a patient, the nature of the ailment and its treatment. What was more disconcerting was that Miss Claye, Miss Masters' successor, recognised and knew the name of every nurse in the entire hospital.

"About 11.30am. Another screened door and Dr MacQueen [presumably one of the two resident doctors] *arrives to do his round. Everything stops. Quiet must be maintained whilst he is with us. He won't stop long as he and the Medical Superintendent cover the whole of the hospital day and night..."* **(DG)**

At some point in the day you had two hours off

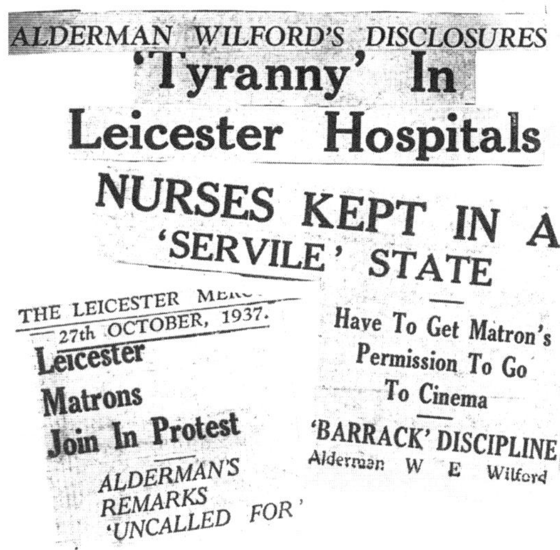
ALDERMAN WILFORD'S DISCLOSURES
'Tyranny' In Leicester Hospitals
NURSES KEPT IN A 'SERVILE' STATE
Have To Get Matron's Permission To Go To Cinema
'BARRACK' DISCIPLINE
Alderman W E Wilford

THE LEICESTER MERC...
27th OCTOBER, 1937.
Leicester Matrons Join In Protest
ALDERMAN'S REMARKS 'UNCALLED FOR'

Public argument over nurses' conditions,1937

and this was arranged daily by the Sister. As a trainee nurse you attended lectures during your two hours - if on nights you got up, attended lectures and remained awake! You returned to your ward until 8pm where *"you take all the counterpanes off for the night and fold them neatly over the bedfoot. Sister says 'Evening Prayer' and it's lights out at 8pm" (PR),* and you handed over to the night staff. You have one day off every week, according to Dora Greaves this was never on Saturday or Sunday, although Miss Stoneley recalls that she only had one day off a month! You did not know until the night before, if you had a day off.

Discipline was exceptionally rigid and detailed, even in such matters as deportment around the buildings - no running, even in an emergency - and not a single hair to show beneath your cap. There was a hierarchy in which each person knew her exact place and it was constantly reinforced. This was accepted both within and between the ranks of nurse, sister, assistant matron, matron, doctors and consultants.

They remained rigidly within their intake group and at meals times each nurse had her allocated place at the table and had to remain in it at all times. Junior nurses were required to serve their seniors before serving themselves, even to interrupt their meal to do this. Meals were supervised by the Assistant Matron who said grace. They were required to open and close doors for their seniors. The irony of this was that she was on equal terms with her former senior once she was qualified.

The tough life of the nurses was tempered by more joyful events and activities. There was considerable camaraderie within each intake and in the hospital there was a variety of events, such as concerts and dances arranged by the staff for staff and patients. They also escaped into the outside world and with permission you could stay out late. To pass in and out of the hospital grounds, unofficially and surreptitiously, you crept past the porter's lodge beneath the level of his window - tactics well known to the sisters and others who had previously done this themselves. Arrangements were made with your immediate colleagues to get you back into the building - *"a string tied to the toe of the one nearest to the door which was pulled vigorously to notify your return".* Being in a nurses home in University Road offered wonderful opportunities:

"...We were in town, and could get up at 4 o'clock and join in all manner of things, for example, the "Tea Dance" at Boots, 4pm - 6pm, admission 6d, which included a cup of tea and a cake. The quartet of very good musicians was excellent and

they would play any tune by request..." ***(DG)***

There was also the Palais de Dance: "[it] *...was a great place for an evening out, with much borrowing of 'finery' from friends for the occasion. There was much 'making and mending' and 'snoods' and long 'bobs' were in. We also had to be in by 10.30pm unless we had a late pass, so there was much climbing in at windows and use of fire escape doors..."* ***(DG)***

On passing their examinations a group celebrated in style: *"...we decided to arrange a meal in town. We would go to Olorenshaw's Fish Restaurant - a very distinguished place. It stood just inside Humberstone Gate near the Clock Tower. Here we could have fish, chips and peas with bread and butter and a cup of tea for a shilling (5p now)... Money was always in short supply, but my mother regularly sent me postage stamps to encourage me to write home regularly and here, I must shamefully admit that I sold some of those stamps to finance my celebration meal at Olorenshaw's. The transport was by tramcar and cost 2d each way..."* ***(DG)***

The City General dealt with all general hospital work. There was also a TB ward - mainly chronic cases which were not accepted at Groby Road and also chronically sick and aged patients - both a legacy of the hospital's Poor Law origins. The nurses referred to this legacy: one remembers the hopeless nature of many of the TB cases, another referred to the condition of the destitute VD diseased girls, many of them expectant mothers. Frances Stoneley notes the incidence of rheumatism amongst young children. She also remembers dealing with families unwilling to accept that a patient was to be sent home. They would also avoid visiting the hospital on the day that the representative from the City Health Department came to collect money for a patient's hospital stay.

The nature of medical care and practice prevailing during this period is of particular interest. The experiences of these nurses confirms and reinforces the accounts of the limited and unchanging medical practice. They all stressed that there were no antibiotics. All referred to the use of sulphonamides, aspirin and derivatives, and the new M&B. Their lists of available drugs were limited and traditional - morphine (used quite extensively), digitalis, mercury, serum (for diphtheria), and even gold solution (in this case for the 'treatment' of syphilis). In addition there were other remedies, many used in the home - liquid paraffin, turpentine, blackcurrant tea (for coughs, made from blackcurrant jam and hot water!), meths, talcum powder, bread and later kaolin poultices. There was considerable reliance upon simple external physical treatments such as the poultices and lotions and ointments to be rubbed on chests and buttocks, inhalers (including steam kettles) and tepid baths. Some of the medical procedures seem arcane, even bizarre, today.

One of the operating theatres had been converted from part of a ward:

"Scrubbed floor... a very large heavy operating table was its centre-piece... 'Scrubbing up' routine - soap, water and brush for five minutes (a clock stood on the window sill), followed by a 'turpentine rub in' and then the hands were dried off with methylated spirit... No gloves for nurses yet!... There was no such thing as a suction pump then, so surgery was usually a very gory affair.

Anaesthesia was little more than 'rag and bottle' with ether chloroform and a Schimmelbusch mask... The patients mostly survived and lived to tell the tale..."

By now the use of X-rays was well established. Blood transfusions were carried out:

"...it was a matter of patient and donor on beds next to each other... direct transfusion... having ensured compatibility of blood. Surprisingly little account was taken of problems of hepatitis..." ***(FS)***

Preparing morphine injections:

"...we had to prepare morphine for injection - glass spirit lamp and matches, teaspoon, syringe and needles, saline solution, sterile water, swabs and skin cleaning lotion. With scrubbed hands the syringe and needle were thoroughly washed in cold saline solution and rinsed out with sterile water. A teaspoon of water was then boiled over the spirit flame and the required amount drawn up into the syringe - remainder discarded. Tablet of morphine then placed in a spoon and covered with the boiled water from the syringe. It soon dissolved with a stir or two from the end of the syringe and was then drawn up again and at last it was ready for administering..." ***(DG)***

Expectant mothers were cared for in antenatal wards. When they went into labour they had to be transferred to the Maternity Unit located away from the main building:

"They had to be transported to the Maternity by bath chair. This was an enormous wicker affair, with very large side wheels and a small front wheel attached to a steering handle, which was supposed to be controlled by the patient. Power was provided by the nurse pushing from the back. During daylight this was always a hazardous task but during the night it was often horrendous and a frightening experience. There was only one lamp on that section of the drive, so as the nurse and her bath chair entourage set off from the main hospital, she was loaned a very large flash lamp. Then Sister O'Hare would go and stand outside Ward 16 on the balcony and continually flash her light until she got the signal that you had arrived..." ***(DG/PR)***

Sister O'Hare spent all her working life at the hospital:

"...Unfortunately her eyesight was failing and she had to wear spectacles, so the checking of drugs became a real trial. To offset this dilemma, every night nurse had to be prepared for sister to stand on the kitchen table directly under the light..." ***(DG)***

We may wonder how the patient recovered from illness and how the nurses especially achieved it:

"It was sheer bed side nursing! If a patient had pneumonia and went into crisis with a high temperature you nursed them until the crisis was over. You might even hold them down." ***(PR)***

One nurse recalls a patient trying to jump off the balcony in a state of delirium. Another talks of prayers being offered *"...Sister fell on her knees by the bed and started praying."* The patient was saved and recovered, *"Prayers of thankfulness to heaven burst forth from the Sister..."* ***(AM)***

Such nursing was protracted and demanding.

A nurse saw patients through illness, crisis, recovery, then into convalescence and a close bond would develop. The nurses interviewed felt that the advent of new medicines, new forms of surgery and medical technology and procedures, and new ways of organising hospitals had changed all this. They welcomed this however as patients recovered more safely and quickly, but it seemed too mechanical to them and it was not their real nursing.

For TB patients at the Groby Road Hospital life was different, mainly because of the nature of the ailment and its treatment. You normally stayed in Groby Road Hospital longer than for most other illnesses. When the first TB wards were opened, this was stipulated in the regulations:

"...(c) Patients are admitted in the first instance for one month only.

(d) At the end of one month, if the case appears to be making satisfactory progress, a second month's stay is granted subject to a payment of 10s per week. If the patient when at work was a subscriber to the Saturday Hospital Society - as so many of the workpeople in Leicester now are - this charge is defrayed by that Society...

(e) At the end of the second month if the case is still making satisfactory progress, a third month's stay is granted free of charge. Occasionally, in special cases a fourth month is granted on payment of 10s per week."

(MOH 1908)

Thus in the early days:

LEICESTER BOROUGH SANATORIUM,

GROBY ROAD.

Regulations for Patients.

All patients (whether insured or non-insured) are admitted to the Sanatorium on the understanding that they will strictly carry out and abide by the following regulations:—

1.—They shall carry out the instructions of the Medical Superintendent and Resident Medical Officer, and, subject to their authority, of the Sister in charge.

2.—They shall not be guilty of any bad language, disorderly or rude behaviour, bad manners, or incivility.

3.—They shall do such work and take such rest and exercise as the Medical Officer shall direct.

(Patients who are fit to do so, are expected to make themselves generally useful and to help the Sister in Charge and Nurses in any way that may be considered desirable. It is in their own interests that they should do this).

4.—They shall conform punctually to the Sanatorium Time Table.

5.—Spitting, except into proper receptacles, is strictly forbidden.

6.—Smoking is only allowed during the specified times, and subject to the discretion of the Resident Medical Officer.

7.—Card playing for money and betting or gambling of any kind are forbidden.

8.—Patients, when out for walks are forbidden to enter any public house, and they shall not receive or consume any alcoholic liquor whilst at the Sanatorium.

9.—Patients shall only be allowed outside the Sanatorium Grounds at such times as the Resident Medical Officer shall determine.

10.—Male and female patients are not allowed to associate with each other either in the Sanatorium grounds or while out for walks.

11.—Any complaints shall be made to the Medical Superintendent or the Resident Medical Officer.

12.—Infringement of any of the Regulations will render the patients liable to be at once discharged. The Medical Superintendent has discretionary power to request any patient to leave who is not in his opinion a suitable patient to remain at the Sanatorium.

C. K. MILLARD, M.D.,
Medical Officer of Health.

Approved by the Sanatorium Sub-Committee,
March 12th, 1913.

Groby Road Sanatorium: regulations for patients, approved prior to its opening in 1914

"...Glass shelters, which serve also as 'sun-traps', have been erected in the grounds, and the open-air treatment is thoroughly carried out. The patients sleep out of doors, on glass covered verandas, winter and summer alike. The patients wait upon themselves, and do most of the necessary ward work, the staff only consisting of one charge nurse - who is necessary to maintain discipline, and to attend to any patient who may be temporarily confined to bed - and one maid. In summer those patients who are fit for it are given, as far as possible, light occupation in the grounds. The patients are allowed at stated times each day to go for a walk outside the hospital grounds, and this

*privilege has rarely been abused." **(MOH 1908)***

It was a spartan existence but there was some joy:

*"...The recreations provided consist of air-gun practice, throwing darts, bagatelle, draughts etc., and gramophone concerts. Recently a small billiard table (kindly lent by Dr. Cox) has been added..." **(MOH 1908)***

By 1914, with the opening of the Sanatorium, a more developed medical treatment yet still spartan regime was introduced:

"As soon as the patient is admitted he is given rest in bed for a day or two in order that he may adjust himself to his new surroundings. When he has settled down he is allowed up and given graduated walks, commencing with about 1/4 mile once or twice daily according to his condition (chest and general) permits. About the end of a week (unless his progress is more rapid) he is allowed to walk 1 - 1 1/2 miles at least per diem and commences No. 1 Breathing Exercises which include systematic expansion of the chest a given number of times twice daily.

"When progressing favourably up to this stage a patient is next put on No. 2 and finally No. 3 Exercises which include graduated Swedish movement with dumbbells, in order not only to develop the chest especially but also to induce a good muscular tone throughout the body and improve posture. The walks are at the same time correspondingly increased in distance, the maximum being about 2 1/2 to 3 miles.

"In order that exercises may be properly supervised, so that a patient does not either under or overdo them, and in order that fresh movement may be taught, thereby keeping up the patient's interest, it has been arranged that they be under the control of an instructor who visits the hospital three times every week, giving instruction to men, women and children, separately.

"On the days when he does not visit, the exercises are gone through under the leadership of the 'captains' of the various wards.

*"These graduated exercises are productive often of very much manifest improvement and are taken up on the whole with no little enthusiasm by the patients themselves who are fully alive to the benefits derived from them..." **(MOH 1914)***

In 1916 the '*Leicester Frith Garden Colony*' was established, which marked a further development in treatment. Selected patients and ex-patients were housed away from the main Sanatorium. They enjoyed certain privileges, a less regimented daily routine, and were even allowed home, subject to medical permission, from Saturday midday to Sunday evening. Patients worked five hours a day in the kitchen gardens of Leicester Frith nearby. Under the supervision of a gardener they produced crops mostly for use in the main hospitals but some were sent to retail shops. The patients were given six pence pocket money a day subject to their satisfactory effort. The scheme was not a success due to poor patient response. There is no further reference to the colony in later reports.

The regime continued to be rather rigid through the 1920's and into the 1930's because "*the enforced discipline is in their interests" **(MOH 1926)***. Further activities were developed to occupy patients and offer rehabilitation:

"...For the patients who are up, it is essential to

provide light work in which they can feel an interest. A few enter with zest into the rural pursuits, pig and poultry rearing, bee-keeping, gardening etc. The greater number find their interest in the varied tasks of the workshop. The introduction of splint and appliance making for the institution has given rise to much interesting light work in aluminium, iron, leather, wood and textiles fabrics. The making of canework baskets, trays, tea-pots stands etc., has occupied many male and female patients throughout the winter. A few have preferred shoe-repairing and have done much good work in this line. Others have produced various light articles in plaster, light metal and wood." ***(MOH 1926)***

Life at the Groby Road Sanatorium
Above: May Jones (later May Elday) seated second right, with fellow patients 1935/36
Below: Frederick Elday (patient 1935-36)

It was considered that:

"...Working with the hands is a wonderful solace to the mind... The cares of home or business melt away from a mind so engaged... Calmness and serenity take their place. With contentment come better appetite and sleep, and a gradual adjustment to the new environment... patients all working together in this spirit, eager to pursue the new handicraft, to exploit the new knowledge... certain problems formerly the bugbear of Sanatorium life find a ready solution... there is... no loafing, and there is no difficulty, except on the rarest occasions with Sanatorium discipline... Co-operation between patient and staff become whole-hearted..." ***(MOH 1931)***

Mrs Jacqueline Bass provides some poignant insights into life at Groby Road through the experiences of her mother and father in 1935-36:

Of the horrors of TB, *"...My Father, Frederick*

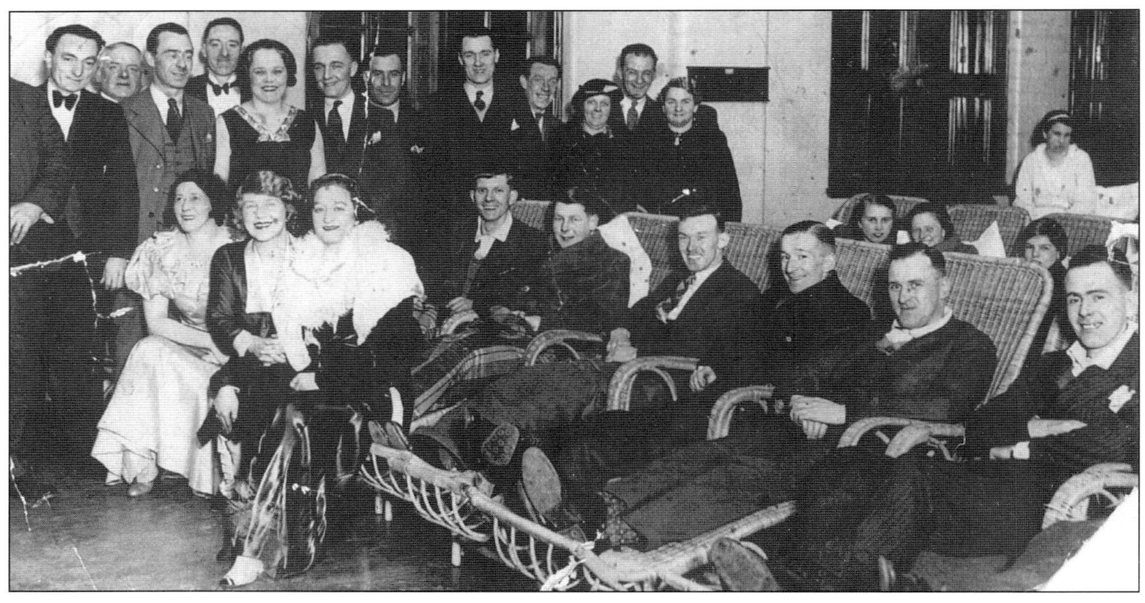

Life at the Groby Road Sanatorium: patients and a visiting concert party 1935-36

Louis Elday, and my Mother, May Jones, met and courted in the then Isolation Hospital. Both were there with tuberculosis which was rife at the time. The drugs that now contain and cure the disease were still in their infancy, so rest, fresh air, diet and isolation were the order of the day not Streptomycin - the antibiotic that later contained the disease. In fact at one stage my Father's lungs were injected with gold dust as a possible cure, he bore the deep scars of the operation on his back all his life..."

Of occupational therapy, *"...local craftsmen would visit to pass on skills to the patients to wile away the hours of a long stay. My father became adept at making bead and gold wire jewellery and also at making lovely pictures with coloured foil, sweet wrappers and black painted glass - as a child I remember a wonderful fire screen which stood in my Grandmother's front room that was made by this technique. It pictures an old-fashioned lady in a garden, I called her 'Mary, Mary, quite contrary'. Mum became accomplished at crochet and embroidery, making cushions, silk handkerchief cases (a thing of the past!) and lace doilies, etc. Some of the goods the patients made were then sold to visitors and relations to earn a little bit of spending money for more materials and the odd bar of chocolate!..."*

On a happier note, *"...Apart from the down side of the illness, it seems from the tales I heard over the years, that it was a happy place, there was a lot of camaraderie amongst patients and the staff caring for them, many lasting friendships were formed and many romances had their beginning there. The social side of the hospital also made for a less dire atmosphere, which must have existed as so many died or were permanently disabled as a result of TB. There were dances, fancy dress parties, whist drives and concert parties, when visiting artists would put on a show for the 'inmates'..."*

Finally there was romance and a happy ending, *"...As I have previously said, my Mum and Dad met and fell in love whilst in Groby Road Hospital, and when Mum was better and she was discharged, it was not long before Dad was too, and they were married in 1938. Dad always said that they were the lucky ones, 'We went out of the front gates and turned left for home. So many went out and turned right and went next door - Gilroes Cemetery'..."*

After you left hospital you might have gone to a convalescent home. If you had been in the Leicester Royal Infirmary or the City General Hospital it was most likely to be run or arranged by the Saturday Hospital Society. If you were in the Sanatorium then there was 'The Holt' in Norfolk. There were homes for adults and children.

These homes were a little more relaxed. The emphasis was upon building up health through nursing care, good food and a healthy physical environment - later they were mostly near the sea. You were unlikely to be completely bedridden and you were soon out of bed. There was greater freedom, with healthy pursuits and social activities, and you might have been allowed to leave the grounds for brief visits. Nevertheless, these were medical establishments with a Matron in daily charge and a Medical Superintendent who had worked in normal hospitals, with all that it implies. Inevitably there were rules and regulations.

Most patients seem to have been well satisfied with their time in these homes as witnessed by the

Desford Hall Convalescent Home: rules for patients adopted in 1905

RULES.

NAME.

1.—The Institution shall be known as the DESFORD HALL CONVALESCENT HOME, and shall be maintained by, and for the benefit of subscribers to the Leicester and County Saturday Hospital Society.

OBJECTS.

2.—The object of the Institution shall be to receive patients, who after illness require a rest and stay in pure air to complete their restoration to health. The Home shall be used for men and boys over fourteen years of age. Every patient must produce a medical certificate stating nature of illness, and notifying that a change of air is necessary.

3.—Cases shall be deemed inadmissible if:—

i.—Recovering from contagious disease, so long as there is danger of infection.
ii.—Suffering from pulmonary consumption.
iii.—Subject to epileptic or other fits.
iv.—Suffering from cancer in an advanced stage.
v.—Suffering from chronic ulcers attended with offensive discharge.
vi.—Requiring constant medical attendance or constant nursing.
vii.—Such other cases as may from time to time be deemed inadmissible by the Committee of Management.

The decision of the Committee as to the eligibility of all cases shall be final.

4.—Patients shall be sent to the Home for a period not exceeding three weeks, excepting such cases for whom a longer stay has been advised by the doctor of the Home, and provided the said extension shall have received the sanction of the Committee of Management.

5.—Patients must come to the Home in a cleanly state, both as to their persons and their clothing, or they will not be received.

6.—Every patient shall pay for his own washing and rail fare to and from the Home, and shall bring with him stout boots for exercise (if possible two pairs), slippers (preferably felt) for indoor use, and a change of linen, which should be marked.

7.—Each patient, if well enough, shall take daily exercise in the open air, weather permitting, at the discretion of the Matron.

8.—The patients will be expected to assist in such light domestic or other work as the Matron shall require.

9.—Each patient shall be liable to make good any damage done by him to the books, crockery, or other property of the Home.

10.—Any patient who shall enter a public house, or procure intoxicating drink, or who shall use improper language, shall be liable to instant dismissal.

11.—Any patient breaking the rules, or disobeying the Matron, shall be liable to be immediately discharged, and any patients feeling that they have any cause of complaint, may state it either personally or in writing to the Secretary or to the Committee at its next meeting.

12.—Wednesday is visiting day, when patients may receive visits from their friends between the hours of 2-30 to 5 in the afternoon.

13.—A copy of these rules will be supplied to each convalescent before admission, and no one can be excused for breaking any rule on plea of not knowing the rules.

BY ORDER OF COMMITTEE.

N.B.—Money and valuables may be left in charge of the Matron, as the Committee cannot otherwise hold themselves responsible.

H. H. WOOLLEY,
Secretary.

Winchester House,
2, Newarke Street,
Leicester.

letters of commendation. However such tranquillity was not always the case. The Superintendent of the Desford Hall Home drew attention to the bad behaviour of a minority of patients in 1913:

"...In an otherwise harmonious report, I regret to sound a discordant note, but feel it my duty to refer to the fact that the conduct of some of the patients during the year was not all that it should be, or what one would expect from men for whom, so much was being done. I would here say at the outset that the cause of the trouble in the main was due to the fact that some patients were admitted who really had no right to come, in other words there was little the matter with them. It can easily be imagined how such patients look on their stay here as more or less a holiday, they cannot appreciate the rules and little restraints which are necessary for sick people, and the proper conduct of an institution like this, and consequently soon begin to break regulations that were made to protect both the comfort and health of patients, and the good name of the Home. I might add, that the conduct of this small section, was by no means condemned more strongly than by the remainder of the patients."

He does not spell out the nature of this bad behaviour.

Patients at Holt Convalescent Home, Norfolk, c.1935-36

Mr Ken Pearce remembers being in Roecliffe Manor in 1930. He was one of six children from a poor family who lived in Curzon Street. He seems to have been a sickly child and suffered a number of illnesses. He can remember having chicken-pox. He was four years old when he was sent to Roecliffe Manor, possibly arranged through the Saturday Hospital Fund:

"They fitted me out with a grey flannel shirt, trousers, boots and socks and we were taken on long walks every day. It was probably a combination of these invigorating walks plus the porridge for breakfast and sausage and mash for dinner which set me on the road to a full recovery."

Roecliffe Manor Convalescent Home for Children
Above: patients out for a walk in Charnwood Forest 1937-8
Below: younger patients, c.1939

Swain Street Institution (later Hillcrest Hospital): Residents of the 'workhouse', the Master is seated in the middle c. late 1890's/early 1900's

Destitute, old and sick!
"The poor are always with us"

There have always been people in Leicester without much money. There were the poor who, for many different reasons, found difficulty in supporting themselves and their dependents. Then there were the paupers, the utterly destitute poor, as well as the vagrants - those with no fixed abode, who needed help from charitable or public bodies in order to survive. All these levels of poverty were complicated by the 'aged and infirm' and the 'chronic sick', who needed total help and even hospital care.

There was no universal financial provision for pension, welfare or health until after the Second World War. The National Insurance Act of 1911 marked the beginning of some provision for certain men. Further legislation in the 1920's and 1930's extended cover for a wider range of people and age-groups. Whilst things had improved during the later 1930's, it was too late and too little for many people. The majority of the destitute, sick and old could only turn to the Poor Law Guardians and their successor the Public Assistance Board, although this latter change did not bring any changes in how you were treated.

There were a few charities in Leicester providing for a limited number of people, the most notable being Trinity Hospital and Wyggeston's Hospital. Other charities catered for very specific groups such as young women and 'fallen' girls, or ex-prisoners.

If you were poor but able-bodied and had somewhere to live, you could seek 'Out-relief'. If you were really a pauper you went into the Swain Street Institution, the 'Workhouse', along with the old and infirm. If you were a vagrant you went to another part of the Workhouse commonly referred to as the 'Spike'. The old who were chronically sick went to the North Evington Poor Law Infirmary. After this became the Leicester City General Hospital such patients went to the workhouse, now renamed as Hillcrest Hospital. Whether it be indoor, that is Workhouse or Infirmary, or out-relief, the conditions for receiving any help were strict and had hardly changed over the fifty years since 1900.

The Poor Law Union dated back to 1836 and was governed by the Board of Guardians. The Guardians were elected on an ad-hoc basis and were mainly middle class business and professional men, but included some women. In 1929 the Poor Law was swept away and replaced by Public Assistance Committees in the counties and county boroughs under the Public Assistance Board. The local authorities became responsible not only for the provision of welfare and health care, but also for the assessment and payment of assistance. This latter responsibility was taken away in the 1940's and given to a renamed Public Assistance Board, leaving local authority committees responsible for the provision of care

LEICESTERSHIRE COUNTY COUNCIL

PUBLIC ASSISTANCE INSTITUTIONS

VISITING OF INMATES

The Public Assistance Committee of the Leicestershire County Council hereby order that the following Regulations shall, in pursuance of Article 69 of the Public Assistance Order, 1930, apply to the Visiting of Inmates of Institutions under their control :—

1. Patients in the Sick Wards and Inmates of other Wards may be visited by relatives and friends during the afternoons of Saturday and Sunday and upon one other afternoon upon such day as the House Committee may appoint, in each week, between the hours of 2 and 4-30 or by special permit of the Head of the Institution at other times.

2. A patient dangerously ill may, unless visitation is prohibited or restricted by the Medical Officer, be visited at any reasonable time.

3. Visits to Sick Wards should in no case be of longer duration than an hour, and may be terminated at any time should it be desirable in the interests of the patient.

4. No more than two persons shall be allowed to visit an inmate at any one time except by special permission of the Head of the Institution.

5. No child under the age of 14 years shall be permitted to visit any inmate unless accompanied by a responsible adult except in cases where, owing to the condition of the patient or other circumstances, (a) the Medical Officer in respect of patients in the Sick Wards, and (b) the Head of the Institution in respect of other Wards, deems it desirable to depart from the regulations. Visiting in Children's Wards or Nurseries by children under 14 years of age shall not be permitted.

6. Visitors shall not pass from Ward to Ward, nor from bed to bed, except by permission of the Officer in charge of the Ward.

7. Visitors are strictly prohibited from smoking inside the Institution.

8. Visitors shall preserve order and quietness whilst in the Institution.

9. Visitors shall not take clothing, spirituous liquors, food, or other articles (with the exception of fruit, flowers, tea, sugar, tobacco, biscuits, cakes, eggs, sweets or butter) into the Institution in any circumstances whatever. Any fruit, flowers, tea, sugar, tobacco, biscuits, cakes, eggs, sweets or butter brought into the Institution for patients or inmates shall be given into the custody of the Officer in charge, who will be responsible for their safe custody, and for seeing that they are given to the patient or inmate at the proper time or times, and in cases of patients in the Sick Wards in accordance with the directions of the Medical Officer.

10. Razors, knives, scissors, or other edged tools, shall not on any account be given to patients or inmates. In cases of infringement of this rule, visitation by the person or persons concerned shall be prohibited forthwith.

11. Visitors are prohibited from making gifts of money to inmates, except with the sanction of the Head of the Institution.

12. Visitors shall be refused admission to the Institution in cases in which visiting has been prohibited by (a) the Medical Officer in cases of patients of Sick Wards, and (b) the Head of the Institution in cases of Other Wards, but in all cases in which visiting has been prohibited in pursuance of this Regulation, such prohibition shall be reported to the next meeting of the House Committee by the responsible Officer by whom such prohibition was ordered.

13. No intoxicated person shall be allowed to enter the Institution.

14. Visitors may be required to take their departure immediately should they be found to be acting in contravention of these regulations or failing to observe due order or otherwise acting in a manner not conducive to the well-being of the inmates of the Institution.

L. Bell & Co. The Guildhall Press, Leicester.

Hillcrest Hospital: notice for visitors, c.1930

only. This explains the various changes in both the use and organisation of hospitals and institutions in Leicester, noted earlier.

The offices of the Board of Guardians and its successor were in a splendid building in Pocklington's Walk. Today they are the offices of the Registrar of Births, Deaths and Marriages. The Swain Street Institution and the North Evington Poor Law Infirmary were also grand Victorian buildings. The former was described by a local newspaper when it was opened in 1839 as:

"...one of the best-looking buildings of that description we have ever seen. The front elevation is particularly judicious, having a neat homely English appearance, and nothing of the character of a Bastille."

These sentiments were not shared by its many occupants over the next 130 or so years. The original buildings of the Infirmary remain at the City General Hospital.

How many people found themselves in the Workhouse and the Infirmary? These would vary according to the state of the local economy. Just prior to the Great War, in the second week of November 1912, there were 822 in the Workhouse. During the war the levels fell to 532 in the second week of January 1917, and there was a further fall by the next year - 381 in early February 1918. The District HM Inspector for the Poor Law, *"...hoped that when the demobilisation took place they would never find old soldiers appealing to the Board for relief. He also hoped that, though they might have some trouble they would soon get back into really prosperous peace times..."* ***(Newspaper report)***

His hopes were fulfilled in numbers in the Workhouse but not so in the case of those receiving out-relief.

Life in the Workhouse was grim and austere, with a highly regulated regime. It seems that Hillcrest was progressive, for it provided married quarters and never separated husband and wife. Everyone was put to work according to their capacity, in the bakehouse, the kitchens, the laundry and the lodge, as well as in domestic duties. There was a farm further out, probably at the North Evington Poor Law Infirmary, which remained in use into the 1960's. The institution had its own shoemaker, tailor, painters, carpenters and even made its own bricks, even up to the early 1950's. There was also a special maternity unit. Over 100 babies were born there in 1905, and it was still in operation in 1939.

A notice for those visiting the inmates shows how strict conditions were. The notice was dated 1930 - after the end of the Poor Law - but its tone could be of the 1890's or earlier! Another notice concerning alcohol on the premises is likewise uncompromisingly severe.

There was a strict timetable for inmates. Breakfast was at 7am (7.30 in winter), milk at 9.30am, 'wines, spirits and other extras' 9.30 - 10.00 - it is presumed that these were allowed and possibly issued at this time. Dinner was at 12 noon, a cup of tea at 4pm and supper was at 5.30pm. Then early to bed!

The diet of the inmates was strictly laid down and could not be varied without permission from the Board of Guardians, even for the provision of a hot-cross bun at Easter! Details of the diet were displayed in the dining hall as late as 1945. The residents were entitled to have their food weighed to check this. A newspaper report of a Board of Guardians meeting gives insights into these strict conditions and the diet in general:

TRIPE AND MARGARINE FOR BEEF AND BUTTER

...Mr Sherriff in moving the report of the House committee, which recommended changes in the dietary at the Workhouse, comprising tripe for meat on one day per week, and margarine for butter, said that the manner in which inmates of the Workhouse had hitherto been supplied with food etc., there might not have been a world war going on at the present time. But the time had now come to face the facts. The butter they supplied to the Workhouse cost 7s 8½ per lb. Making a total outlay of £21 7s 6d per week, against the cost of £10 15s per week in pre-war times when it cost 10½d per lb. Further, in pre-war times they could send back the butter if not up to quality but now they had to take it and keep it, whether good, bad or indifferent. After six months of experiment he was persuaded that the best margarine was preferable to a large proportion of so-called butter at present on the market for which they pay extortionate prices (Hear, hear). Allowing for a 20 per cent increase in the cost of margarine, they could buy what was required for £11 11s per week, which would effect a saving of £9 16s 6d per week. They were effecting a saving of 30s per week on milk by using condensed milk for tea and coffee, and with regard to the proposal to substitute tripe for meat on one day a week, this would effect a saving of £6 14s 2d on the one meal for the Workhouse. In doing this they would be able to substitute 250lbs of tripe for 220lbs of beef. For the beef they paid 1s 3d per lb and for one week at the house it cost £13 15s, against £7 1s 11d for tripe. If tripe suppers were so good, added Mr Sherriff facetiously, there could be no doubt that a tripe dinner would be excellent, and he thought that inmates would welcome the change on one day per week.

Miss Leeson warned the Board that a brand of margarine which was being greatly pushed was a Dutch brand. Just as good an English brand could be obtained, and she thought this ought to be done.

Councillor Salt mentioned that margarine was used at the Borough Mental Hospital for patients, staff, and doctors alike, and all were well satisfied with it.

Mr Martin, vice-chairman, opposed the suggestion of substituting margarine for butter, though he did not oppose the substitution of tripe for beef. So long as they could get butter they should have it.

Mr Holland said he was a convert to margarine. Formerly he opposed it, but it was then a different article. It was a fat. They had come to the time when they might follow the example of other large institutions and many private persons and substitute margarine for butter.

Mr Sherriff, in reply to a question, said he hoped that the new dietary, if adopted, would apply to officials as well as inmates. It must be remembered that the soldiers today train on it, and a large proportion of the people of the country also used it.

On being put to the meeting, the resolution was carried almost unanimously...'

(Newspaper report January 1917)

Vagrant numbers at the Workhouse varied quite dramatically, for example there were 196 in the institution in the second week of November 1912, and 197 in mid-January 1921. Normally the figure seems to have been around seventy or eighty. Nevertheless concern was expressed from time to time with regard to high vagrant numbers. Thus in 1927 the District Inspector responsible for the Poor Law in the East Midlands reported:

"Leicester appears to be the main tramp centre in the district. During the quarter ending 31st March 1927, the following were admitted: 4348 men, 145 women and 11 children. Of these, 2651 men, 60 women, and 2 children were detained two nights. There were transferred to the Infirmary 45 men. Of the total numbers 262 men and 16 women were over 65 years of age, sick and infirm under 65 numbered 174 men and 15 women."

Conditions for the vagrants were possibly marginally worse than for the other inmates. An insight into this is a report following an official visitor's visit.

...A record in the visitors book was to the effect that the male sleeping accommodation was 'a disgrace to the Board'.

Miss Mackintosh who was one of the visitors in question said one point she objected to was that vagrants who had been in the house the previous day had to go to bed at 5 o'clock. She would also like the males to have straw mattresses as well as the females, and, personally, she did not like the heating arrangements. Warmth was wanted for their feet, but the hot water pipes were at the head....

Mr Walter Smith observed that if Miss Mackintosh knew so much about the vagrant war as other members did she would not have brought that complaint forward. As to heating apparatus, how many of the tramps enjoyed such benefits when they were on the road? So far as the bedding was concerned, he thought Miss Mackintosh wanted eider-down quilts (Laughter).

Mr Tomlin said the five o'clock rule had now been suspended for eight o'clock. He could not agree about the sleeping accommodation. From enquiries he had made he was led to believe that the accommodation generally was superior to any in the country and the tramps were well looked after and humanely treated. (Hear, hear)
The resolution was lost...
(Newspaper report July 1920)

Another newspaper report tells us something about the provision of meals:

PROPOSED 'WAR' DIETARY FOR VAGRANTS

...A letter was received from the Leicestershire Vagrancy Committee stating that in accordance with the request of the Food Controller they had revised the dietary, and asked the Board to accept the same and put it into operation.
The Chairman said that in the proposed dietary there is no reduction in the case of children. The bread allowance had been reduced for females from 6oz to 2½oz and for men from 8oz to 2½oz for supper and either 1lb of boiled rice or a pint of broth or porridge substituted. The bread for dinner was reduced to 4½oz.
(Newspaper report March 1917)

There does, by contrast, seem to have been a more humane and kindly aspect. One young soldier's wife, in a letter to the Infirmary Committee of the Board of Guardians, expressed gratitude for the help she had received:

I hope you will forgive the liberty I am taking but it is the only way I can think to express my gratitude. I have got my little one, Robert Crofts,

Hillcrest Hospital 1950's. Above: facilities for itinerants
Right: individual rooms for itinerants
Below: dormitory for itinerants

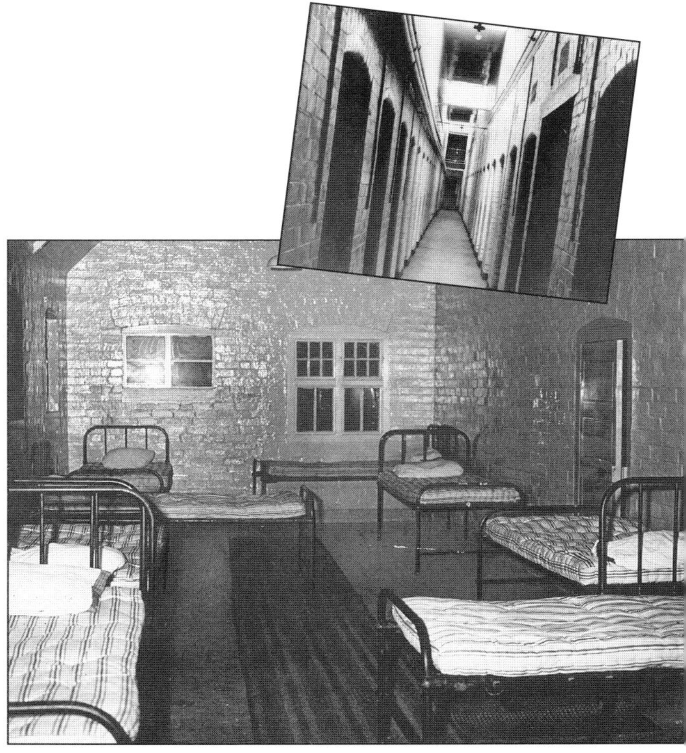

back home again. You will remember Mr Stokes got him admitted into the Poor-law Infirmary about four months ago, when he weighed about 11lb., I believe, and was getting thinner each week. I kept taking him to the Royal Infirmary and to the Baby Depot each week, but nothing I did at home made any difference, in fact I am sure he would have died at home. He was the most miserable child I had seen; for a long time he was pining away. He now weighs 1st 8lb 4oz and is only 1 year old, so you will understand why I am so pleased. He is not only fat and hard, but they have turned him into a healthy, bonny, and roguish little scamp. I shall do all I can to make it known what the dear kind nurses are doing at the Poor-law Infirmary, as I am afraid it is rather overlooked, and they do not get much of the big print; but it may be some consolation to them to know my husband says "They are worth fighting for who are caring for the soldiers' children".
(Newspaper report November 1917)

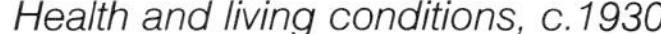
Health and living conditions, c.1930

Conditions for the receipt of out-relief were as harsh and unyielding as being in the Workhouse. Numbers receiving out-relief fluctuated over relatively short periods. In the first week of November 1912 there were 3086 on out-relief, costing the Guardians a total of £464 11s 3d, an average of 3s (15p today). The numbers fell steadily during the Great War - 2558 in June 1916, 1850 in February 1918 and they continued to fall even after the war - as low as 1604 in January 1921. During the war most of the local fit men were in the Armed Forces, so the demands of the war effort provided job opportunities for the unemployed and the less fit. During 1921 the numbers increased dramatically reaching a peak of 5094 in the second week of October, reflecting the collapse of the national and local economy. The amounts disbursed by the Guardians followed these variations, the average amount per person increased, reflecting the cost of living rather than generosity on their part - by May 1924 it averaged 6s $7\frac{1}{2}$d (about 36p).

Out-relief was given in kind as well as money through the issue of food or tickets for specific products:

ISSUE OF COAL TICKETS

In accordance with notice of motion Mr Bedford proposed the adoption of the system of issuing coal tickets to recipients of out-relief. He said he had, the other Sunday, visited 30 homes of those in receipt of out-relief, and found that seven of them had no fires, and if the Board knew all the circumstances he had no doubt they would pass the motion. In another district three out of 12 homes were without fires.

Supposing two old people, aged 68 and 69 were in receipt of 10s relief and their rent came to 3s 6d,

they would only have 6s 6d a week left over for food, light and coal. He wanted the Board to give committee power to grant a bag of coal in cases where they considered it necessary... (Eventually the motion was carried).
(Newspaper report November 1916)

After discussion, it was agreed to resume the distribution of bread to the out-door poor as formerly, but to give money in lieu of tea and sugar, it being stated that in present circumstances it was no advantage to the poor to get the allowance in kind.
(Newspaper report May 1919)

Two cases are worth quoting at some length as they reflect the problems of getting out-relief and the long arguments within the Board of Guardians:

The Leicester Board of Guardians at its meeting last night vetoed a proposal of one of the relief committees to pay 10s a week out-relief to a widow with seven children who contributed nearly £4 a week between them to the family exchequer... Mr Bedford chairman of the committee concerned, said the case had given them some little trouble, but they felt that the needs of the woman at the moment should be met. The seven children between them gave their mother £3 19s a week. The committee had, in view of that, reduced the 18s which they had previously allowed her to 10s. One of the sons had been in the Service, and after demobilisation he received the Government allowance of 29s out of which he gave his mother £1. Then he obtained work, and gave his mother 32s a week. He moved that they should allow the woman 10s...
Mr West said that according to his figures the total income of the family was £6 14s 10s a week and the mother only received £3 19s of that. "Now, gentlemen" said Mr West "if you think that is a case of destitution, I do not".
Mr Hancock contended that it could not be said that the children were not paying their quota.
Mr D.G. Holland said there was another view, and that was what did parents do for the children in bringing them up? The responsibility in this case was on the children.
Mr Harrison urged that it was not a question of 79s a week being adequate. For argument's sake, they would say that it was not. The question was, who was to make up the deficiency? Was it to be the elder sons and daughters of the woman or the elder sons and daughters of some other family? He was quite satisfied that it was the duty of the eldest son in this case...
(Newspaper report July 1920)

The same edition of the newspaper in a leading article entitled 'A bad sign of the times' commented:

...The case is one of many instances that have come to the front lately of a loss of family self-respect. Time was, not so very long ago, when children would have made any sacrifices to keep their parents, or any one dear to them, "off the rates". To-day, if one may trust many evidences, sons and daughters shirk self-sacrifice. There are cases of course, when it is no disgrace for a citizen to "go on the rates" and we should deplore that any person out of false pride, should undergo severe suffering rather than accept assistance from a fund in which in his (or her) day he (or she) has contributed to. But all of us ought to feel the utmost reluctance in accepting from others assistance, for ourselves and

for our relatives, until we are driven to it. Is the fine old spirit of independence dead?
(Newspaper report July 1920)

The debate on the second case was particularly acrimonious:

STORMY SCENES

Leicester Guardians & Out-Relief Cases

WHAT IS ADEQUATE SUPPORT

Stormy scenes were witnessed at the meeting of the Leicester Board of Guardians held last night, when some appeals were heard against decisions of the Out-Relief Committee.

Miss Fortey instanced the case of a consumptive man and his wife who had now six children. A few months ago they were allowed 55s per week, but since then the sixth child had been born, and the Committee had cut down their relief to 50s.

Mr J.L. Harrison: The committee have fined the parents 5s for having another baby.

Miss H. Leeson said that £3 all but three pence was being received by this married couple. She thought it was not right that these consumptive people should keep having children. Their children would be poor and weakly.

Mr J.L. Harrison remarked that it was a scientific fact that the majority of children born of consumptive parents were healthy provided they had proper food.

Miss Leeson further said that the children never had a chance to live. The least cold would affect them.

CREATING A PRECEDENCE

Another member said that the man would never be able to earn the amount given in out-relief to him by the Board. It would create a precedent. It was not a great victory —

AN UPROAR

At this point there was an uproar, many people trying to speak from the Conservative benches. A voice said that if Mr Martin brought politics into that Board he would have some back.

Mr Martin: They object to being congratulated

Mr J.D. Holland: He wants educating

Mr Vickers: The boot is on the other leg.

Miss Fortey, in reply to a question, said the children's ages were 10, 9, 7, 4 and 2 years, and 3 months.

Miss Leeson: How can you call children of 4 and 2 years and 3 months persons?

Mr Brookes said they must get down to rock-bottom facts. After deducting 7s 6d National Health Insurance from the £3 per week, there was the magnificent sum of 6s 5d per head left. Then rent had to be paid, and light and heat allowed for. Many people spend more than 6s 5d per week on keeping a dog, much less a human being. How could they expect these children to be healthy and fit if the Board took away the five shillings. It was a discredit to the Board.

Mr Tomlin said many people who were working had to struggle along on 50s per week, and they had to help pay for out-relief. Was it fair? Was it right? The Board had to be just as well as generous.

Upon being put to the vote 16 voted for and 12 against Miss Fortey's resolution against the reduction...

(Newspaper report November 1924)

What was it like for the staff working at Hillcrest? As with ordinary hospitals there was a strict regime as well as a clear hierarchy. The Institution was headed by the Master and Matron (ideally a nurse/midwife) who were responsible to the Board of Guardians. They ruled with a rod of iron not just the inmates but also the staff, which consisted of a number of nurses with others responsible for the various facilities and the good order of the place. A lot of work was done by the inmates.

Around the turn of the century there was only a handful of nurses. There was a book of rules covering behaviour as well as their dealings with inmates and others - *'complaints will be avoided'*, leave of absence - strictly at the discretion of the superintendent:

TIME TABLE FOR NURSES AND PROBATIONERS

BREAKFAST AND PRAYERS	*7am to 8am*
WARDS	*8am*
DINNER	*12.30 to 1.30pm or 1.30 to 2.30pm*
TEA	*4 to 4.30pm or 4.30 to 5pm*
SUPPER	*8 to 8.30pm or 8.30 to 9pm*
BEDROOMS	*10pm*
LIGHTS OUT	*10.45pm*

During the 1930's, Hillcrest had expanded its hospital work, following the transfer of patients when the North Evington Poor Law Infirmary became the City General Hospital. Nurses then worked 113 hours a fortnight. By 1939 there were 110 staff, rising to over 200 by 1949.

Life could be cruel for the staff if they broke the rules:

GUARDIANS PIQUED

Official Marries Without Permission

WIFE NOT TO VISIT HIM

Drastic action by the Leicester Workhouse Visiting Committee towards a young official who had married without the consent of the Guardians, was reported at a meeting of the Board held last night, under the chairmanship of Mr T.E. Hassell.

The Committee reported that one of the officials having married without notifying the committee, it was decided that the wife should not be allowed to visit her husband at the workhouse...

Mr Harrison desired to enter an emphatic protest against such action. It appeared, he said, that this official had actually had the audacity to get married without first asking permission. He understood that so strong was the feeling against this man at the committee meeting it was moved, seconded, and very nearly carried that the officer in question be given three months notice for his terrible offence. Instead of that, they had forbidden the wife to visit her husband at the workhouse. It was, said Mr Harrison, with strong emphasis, the inalienable right of everyone to get married if he wished, and it was a piece of rank impertinence on the part of the Guardians to interfere at all, much less to prohibit the wife visiting her husband ("Hear, hear" from several ladies).

They ought to alter conditions of service said Mr Harrison. In asylums there were married quarters, why not in the workhouse?

Mr Kinder asked if any reason could be given for such a prohibition.

Mr Tomlin replied that the committee considered such visits to be undesirable. The report was adopted...

(Newspaper report June 1921)

Countesthorpe Cottage Homes: No. 11 Cottage, c.1920 (now demolished)

Young, destitute and abandoned
"Look upon a little child"

If you were young and destitute for some reason, as with the old and destitute, you would possibly become the responsibility of the Poor Law Guardians or the Leicester Corporation after 1930. Initially you would go into the Receiving Home in Mill Hill Street in Leicester. Then you would go to one of the Scattered Homes or to the Countesthorpe Cottage Homes. It is not clear how the decision was made, it might have been the availability of places at the Cottage Homes or whether your situation was long-term or temporary. Babies and very young children were usually kept in the Workhouse until they were two years old.

The Scattered Homes involved being sent to foster parents and the number of children in such homes varied. In the first week of November 1912 there were 65 children in such homes, by late January 1917 the numbers had risen to 94, possibly arising from men being away in the war. In subsequent years the numbers reverted to pre-war levels. We have little information about life in these foster homes.

Most children went to the Countesthorpe Cottage Homes:

"The Parish of Leicester Cottage Homes, situated about three quarters of a mile west of the village were built in 1884, at a cost, including 55½ acres of land, of £27,000, and consists of 11 cottages, superintendent's residence, infirmary, isolation block, school, workshops and swimming bath; they will hold about 260 children and are managed by a committee of 24 of the guardians, who attend the homes every month; nine homes have 24 children and two 16 children, a foster mother being in charge of each; five of the principal boys' homes have also foster fathers, who are industrial trainers; the infirmary contains 20 beds and the isolation wards 10; divine service is held in the school room on sunday afternoon at 3 o'clock."
(Kelly's Directory, 1928)

The motto of the homes was:

"Good, better, best
never let it rest,
till your good be better
and your better best."

As with all Poor Law institutions the regime was very strict and highly regulated under the daily control of the Superintendent and Matron, yet with constant vigilance and involvement from the Board of Guardians committee. Prevailing attitudes deliberately isolated such children from mainstream local life, as reflected in the location of

Countesthorpe Cottage Homes: the former residence of the Superintendent and Matron

the Homes. The change from Poor Law Guardians to local authority control in 1930 did not lead to any significant shift in the regime.

A book of rules '*General Regulations as to the management of the Homes and Instructions to the Fathers and Mothers*' issued in 1923, set out in minute detail how the Homes would be run. Though they were mostly concerned with children, there were rules covering the duties and lives of the house mothers and fathers:

"You will have charge of the home in which you reside, and for all domestic purposes of the children in the home. It is your duty to be to these children as their Father or Mother, to care for them and train them rightly.

"Whilst you are allowed a large amount of liberty in the management of your Home, yet the Superintendent and Matron are primarily responsible for the management of the 'Homes' and any instructions from them must be implicitly obeyed. Any infringement of the rules must be reported to the committee."

The following all embracing rule went further:

"It is not necessary to define what should be the particular employment of any officer out of the Home or Workshop. You will devote yourself to such work as may be assigned you, always remembering that each one connected with the Homes is ready to act according as there may be a necessity, and to object to any special work is not being in his place to do it."

Staff relationships with both outsiders as well as with fellow staff were clearly circumscribed:

"You are not to be absent from the premises without the knowledge of the superintendent or Matron. A book is kept at the Lodge, in which every person entering or leaving the establishment is required to leave their names entered, and also the time of going out and coming in. This applies to visitors as well. Officers wishing to be out after 10 p.m. must obtain special leave from, and report their return to, the Superintendent or Matron.

"Officers wishing to have a friend to stay for one night must obtain the sanction of the Superintendent or Matron, and all Officers wishing to have friends staying with them for a longer period than one night, must make application to the Superintendent or Matron who will lay the same before the Committee and first obtain consent thereto.

"Visitors must not be invited to come during the forenoon, as a person who has a number of children to look after ought to have enough to occupy all her time till after the dinner hour at least.

"Officers wishing to visit each other must do

so when off duty and between the hours of three and four in the afternoon, and nine and ten at night.

"The evening being the chief period when the children are all at home, the parents are expected to be with them, and instruct them in sewing and other matters pertaining to Home life.

"You will be allowed an average of one and a half days off duty per week, and will not otherwise absent yourself from the premises without the previous knowledge and consent of the Superintendent." (In reality something of a nonsense given the duties.)

If the regulations for staff were tough, those for the children were even more stringent, covering every eventuality and stage of life from the day they arrived to the day they left. It made nonsense of the supposed *"large amount of liberty in the management of your Home"* given to House Mothers and Fathers.

The daily timetable formed the basic structure of life for the children and thereby the staff. It was a long and arduous day which included school and work but also household chores. The weekends would not have school or workshops, but there were still the household chores. Sunday was marked by church services and suitable recreation - invariably a walk in summer with Mother and Father, or the reading of books approved and provided by the Homes.

There was a fixation with cleanliness, in part justified given the problems of disease etc.:

- *"heads are to be regularly examined and combed at least twice a week."*
- *"before being sent to work or school, every child in your Home is to be inspected by you as to cleanliness of person, clothing, boots cleaned, laces tidy, hair and clothes brushed etc."* (The Schoolmaster was provided with a book to record and report any such deviation)
- *"Once a week at least (Friday evening, and oftener if possible) all the children are to have a warm bath at home, and be thoroughly washed under the personal supervision of the Father or Mother, who must be present while the children are being bathed..."*
- *"No child is to wear any clothing belonging to any other child's suit; great attention is to be paid to this, to prevent the spread of disease..."*

Conditions were even laid down on the cutting of hair:

"A Hair-cutter attends monthly, and when required, to cut the children's hair, and it is not to be cut at any other time without the consent of the Superintendent or Matron."

There were also rules for the children's clothing:

"You will see that the children's clothes are kept in proper repair. All the clothing should be repaired in the Homes... When repairs are needed to the boots and shoes, or to the boys' suits, the articles are to be sent in a cleanly state to the Shoemaker's or Tailor's Shops ...at the appointed time, and an order obtained from the Superintendent... All the children must be taught to mend their own clothing, and knit and darn their own stockings."

When working in the home: *"Children should be made to use Kneelers while they are scrubbing, as it is injurious to them and to their clothes to do without, and they are specially obtained for this purpose. Coarse aprons must be used by the House children to protect their clothes..."*

Considerable space is devoted to the feeding

of the children. Rules laid down exact quantities of food and times when stores would be collected. Meals were to be well prepared by the Mother although it was laid down in some detail how many meat dinners as well as pudding, soup etc. would be served, and whether it be a hot or cold meal: *"A cold dinner may be given on Sunday during the hot weather, to avoid unnecessary Sunday labour".* There were rules on use of crockery, with cups and saucers being used on Sundays instead of mugs. All the household had to be present in the dining room unless ill, including both Mother and Father, at breakfast and tea.

Changes in diet could only be determined by the Board of Guardians:

AN EGG ONCE A YEAR

Leicester Guardians and Cottage Homes Children

Although in six months 4730 eggs were produced at the Cottage Homes, Countesthorpe Farm, and were sent to the Swain-street Institution, Mr Harrison, at last evenings meeting of the Leicester Guardians, stated that the children at the Homes never got an egg. It wasn't on the dietary. "I am wrong," said Mr Harrison, "they get an egg once a year, and that on Easter Sunday". He proposed that the children should have one egg per week after next February. The Board agreed to Mr Harrison's motion subject to the consent of the Ministry of Health.

(Newspaper Report November 1923)

Central to life at the Homes was the relationship between the children and the House Mothers and Fathers, especially with regard to discipline and wider behaviour:

"You are not allowed to inflict corporal punishment on the children, or deprive them of their food, but trust to a kindly and firm control and treatment of them, rather than to any system of severity, and by good example and checking small faults, avoid the occurrence as far as possible of serious misbehaviour, but if any serious case of misconduct occurs, it should be reported at the time to the Superintendent or Matron who will give such instructions as they may deem advisable.

"In all your dealing with the children preserve a good temper, as you will have much to try you, many annoyances to put up with, and occasions requiring much firmness. Never allow yourself to speak a word in the hearing of the children that would cause them to treat you or any other officer with disrespect."

Underpinning this was a strong Christian morality. On Sunday there were services in the school room or at the Parish Church or chapel:

"As head of a Christian household, you must read prayers and have them said by the children before breakfast and after supper each day, and have grace said before and after meals, by all the children."

In addition to prayer and church services, moral education was inculcated through approved 'improving' books and through the school curriculum. Domestic duties, keeping beds, clothes and rooms in good order and keeping yourself clean and tidy were seen as a means of developing good behaviour.

The location and self-sufficiency of the Homes ensured the isolation of the children from the wider community. This was reflected in rules with regard to visits:

COTTAGE HOMES

MAXIMUM TABLE FOR STORES.

The Fathers or Mothers are to make out their List of Articles of Food required for the Week for their Home every Monday Morning, and send it to the Superintendent *by 9 a.m.*

The quantities in such List *must not be more* than given in the Tables below, for the number of Children actually in the Home at that time, and *as much less as they require*, having due regard to the *avoidance of waste*. This scale represents the maximum allowance, but does not entitle the Superintendent to issue, or any Officer to demand, the quantities set forth unless required for actual consumption.

Store Baskets must be sent with the Bags for Provisions to the Stores by 9 o'clock every Tuesday Morning, and every alternate Tuesday again, at 2 p.m., for Necessaries.

Meat Baskets must be sent to Stores by 9 o'clock every Friday and 2 p.m. Tuesdays, and Fish Baskets every alternate Friday Morning by 9 o'clock. Potato Skips every Friday by 9 o'clock.

ARTICLES OF FOOD.

Number of Children.	Boys. Bread.	Girls. Bread.	† Flour.	Boys. Meat.	Girls. Meat.	Suet.	Milk.	Potatoes & other Veg.	Peas or Lentils	Drip-ping.	Butter.
	lbs.	lbs.	lbs.	lbs. oz.	lbs. oz.	lbs.	pints.	lbs.	lbs.	ozs.	lbs.
1	7	6	½	1 2	0 14	2 oz.	5	6	1 oz.	2	4 oz.
Rations of Father	6	..	1	4 0	..	¼	3½	7	..	..	½
„ Mother	6	..	1	4 0	..	¼	3½	7	..	..	½

Number of Children.	Lard.	* Cheese.	Oat-meal.	Rice.	Sugar.	Loaf Sugar.	Tea.	Cocoa.	Cur-rants.	Jam or Treacle.	Alternative Weeks: Bacon.	Alternative Weeks: Fish.	Eggs.
	lbs.	lbs.	lbs.	lbs.	lbs.	lbs.	ozs.	ozs.	lbs.	lbs.	lbs.	ozs.	
1	1 oz.	2 oz.	¼	3 oz.	½	..	¼	2	2 oz.	3 oz.	4 ozs.	6	1
Rations of Father	..	½	..	½	½	¼	4	..	¼	..	1	..	4
„ Mother	..	½	..	½	½	¼	4	..	¼	..	1	..	4

NOTE.—Children of Officers who are paid for are allowed half Father's Rations.

A good Housekeeper will, as far as possible, always have a small store of Provisions in the House to meet any extra requirements which may arise, and any mistake in the Stores given out must be reported at once, otherwise it cannot be rectified.

Officers are allowed also 2 ozs. Coffee in lieu of 1 oz. Tea.

The allowance of Meat is for Boys 18 ozs., for Girls 14 ozs. per week. Every alternate week 8 ozs. Fish may be substituted for 2 ozs. Meat.

The allowance of Meat for Officers is 4 lbs. per week. Every alternate week 3½ lbs. Meat and 1 lb. Fish may be substituted for the 4 lbs. Meat.

Officers' Rations are provided for their own consumption on the premises only.

*Cheese for Children over 10

†Except that if required each child may be given up to a maximum of ¾ lb. per week.

Countesthorpe Cottage Homes: food quantities and rules for House Mothers and Fathers, 1923

"No relatives or friends of the children are to be allowed to visit the children without the permission of the Superintendent or Matron. Special days are set apart for this purpose, and then its is only permitted in the school room. The Fathers and Mothers are not to hold any communication whatsoever with the relatives or friends of the children, or allow them to enter any Home."

It was in education and the school environment that the separateness and isolation was most poignant. The Cottage Homes had their own schools for children up to the upper Standard.

Then they went to local schools. Later the younger children also went to local schools. When the Homes were transferred to the City Council the children were bussed to schools in the city - notably Granby Road, Hazel Street, Lansdowne Road and Narborough Road.

They were often resented and treated badly by teachers, parents and children, particularly at the local village schools. In the city schools they seem to have been treated better, though they stood out because of their dress and demeanour. One cruel feature was that the children were often referred to by staff at the Homes, and sometimes by the teachers, by their official number rather than by their name. This did not engender self-esteem!

TREATED WITH CONTEMPT

Mr Gilbert believed that the children who were sent to the County Schools were treated with contempt, and were not wanted.

Mr Hancock said it was true that the children were subject to jeers, and instead of the education being to their advantage it was greatly to their disadvantage. The children sent out from Countesthorpe were sullen, stubborn, ungracious and ungrateful, and were lacking in spirit and personality. He wanted the Cottage Homes to be at least as good as the Desford Industrial School, educationally.

Mr Ellicock agreed that the children sent to the County Schools were treated with contempt. They were jeered at and taunted. They become embittered for life by the treatment, and that led to class hatred. The children at the Homes were the flotsam and jetsam of society, and the Guardians wanted to make them decent citizens. Withdrawing them from the county schools was a step in that direction...

(Newspaper report on meeting of Guardians, November 1924)

In a newspaper report two years earlier, Mr Davey, the Headmaster of the village school noted the behaviour of some children from the Homes:

...as abnormal; vicious and of a type utterly unfitted to attend a village school. He complained of acts of wilful damage committed by them, and of annoyance to various persons on their way to and from school... the children from the Homes set the village children a bad example, and some of the parents would withdraw their children if those from the Homes continued to attend. They had no notion of school discipline, and hindered the progress of other children... Mr Hagon warmly protested against the terms Mr Davey had applied to the children from the Homes, accused him of partiality...

(Newspaper Report July 1922)

A pupil at Hazel Street School in the 1940's describes the separateness of the children in more gentler terms:

"The Countesthorpe children were always there in the school but, looking back, never part of it. They were always recognisable by their uniform appearance - the boys all wore the same dull coarse trousers - short in those days - jerseys with collars, and black boots. They had very short hair cuts - the sort that became fashionable in the 1980's. They always had the same look about them. The girls had a similar uniform sort of look - in winter they wore a navy, possibly serge, dress varied only by contrasting braid on the collars - yellow, red, light blue or green.

Whilst in lessons, apart from their dress, they were part of the class and school but you never made friends with them - they were apart from us. You were always reminded that they were 'different' - just before lunch-time and at the end of the school day, a monitor came into the class room to announce that Countesthorpe children were to go out to their bus - a Leicester City double decker - they went all the way to Countesthorpe and back for lunch. For us local children, these children went off to a mysterious place somewhere." ***(CH)***

This separateness and isolation went further with questions as to the ability of the children to cope with the outside world. It was suggested that the school leaving age of 14 should be rescinded in their case:

...Councillor Sherriff pointed out that the children at Countesthorpe were in a totally different position to ordinary children. At Countesthorpe the children were practically never outside the "ring fence" and they knew nothing about the world. To put another two years on the school life of children under such condition would be very detrimental to them. The committee already had power to deal with special cases, and children should be kept at school for longer periods if desired.
(Newspaper report March 1919)

Reinforcing this were the views of some in authority with regard to the educational standards and achievements of the children. In discussing a Report by His Majesty's Inspector of Schools about the school at the Homes, Miss Leeson stated:

...There was an exceptional number of sub-normal. At least 30 to 33 per cent were one or three years behind their proper standard. Another great difficulty was the dull mentality of many of the children, there was very little retentiveness and no responsiveness to general questioning. Of the 20 children who comprised that standard last spring, only eight could be classed as being in any way normal... (Newspaper report November 1924)

What happened to the children when they left the Homes? Some were there for only a few years and returned to their families once their circumstances had improved. Many however remained until they reached school leaving age. The girls were trained to enter domestic service of some kind. In their later years they were trained by the Matron in her house 'The Residence'. The boys were trained for working in farming and in certain craft trades. Training was undertaken in the Home's own workshops and on its farm, by the House Fathers who were employed for their trades and skills as well as being fathers.

What are the memories of those who were in the Homes? How were the children really treated? Much depended upon which House you were in, who were your Mother and Father, and who were the Superintendent and Matron. Some have fond memories and few regrets, but others regarded their experiences with horror. All agree that life in the Homes was tough and unremitting:

"...I had some good times in the Homes. We played in the bedroom - hanging off the beams and we did concerts and pantomimes and I liked that... Its funny how some children got on all right at the Homes and how some had a terrible time..." ***(Girl, resident 1937 - 45)***

"...The Homes were tough. They taught you with a

rod and they kept you working... At the end of the day though, we were well looked after. They clothed and fed us, even during the war when times were hard... The discipline was harsh, but that's how it was then and my house father, Mr Jackson, was a good man..."
(Boy resident 1937-45)
Despite his view he ran away!

One girl resident (circa late 1930's, early 40's) does not share these views:

"They called us 'Scum of the earth! You're nothing, you're nothing - you've got nothing so you are Nothing, nothing nothing, but scum, scum, scum'!"

At the daily routine level there was the harshness and rigidity. Many accounts refer to food, clothes, general life and school:

"Life in the cottage was hard. We were in Number 10. We used to have to sit on hard benches - hands behind our backs and no talking, and we all had to work. I had to dust and polish and I hated it and rebelled. My sister always looked after me and tried to stop me getting into trouble but I'd say 'I don't care - she's not being fair'. They used to hit us with long bath brushes."
(Girl, resident 1923-37)

"I suppose things were getting better with the new superintendent. We even had different clothes, shoes not boots, and instead of the awful combinations with splits up the back, we had knickers with elastic in the legs. They were thick and navy blue, but they were good to put things in - like sago and tapioca pudding! When we had them, it made me feel sick and I'd wait until the House Mother wasn't looking, then it would go up my knicker leg until I could throw it away. And boiled onions - Ugh! - I couldn't bear them. I've had a lot of boiled onions in those knickers and even more sago pudding - of course you had to keep them round the side so they didn't get squashed..." ***(Girl, resident 1923-37)***

"...but at Countesthorpe it was all the same - panamas in summer, berets in winter. All of us girls wore combinations, vests, navy blue knickers and thick black stockings. Everything itched, vest, knickers, 'combs'. I used to hide the combs and the vest under my mattress and one day the House Mother found it, 'What's this, what's this? Put them on straight away'. So I had to, but it was straight back under the mattress the next day..."
(Girl, resident 1940-42)

"We weren't allowed any toys then - we played with bits of leaves. I was given a doll once - I don't remember by who, but my House Mother took it away from me and I never saw it again. That was when we first got there, but a new superintendent came and after we'd been there a year or so things changed. One Christmas we were told to ask what we wanted from Father Christmas and I asked for a jewellery box. I never thought I'd get anything, but on Christmas morning there was this box and inside were necklaces and rings and shiny bracelets..." ***(Girl, resident 1923-37)***

The same resident talking about school:
"I went to Granby Road School, then to Narborough Road. Everyone looked at us because our clothes had numbers on them, on the outside in a big letter. I was number 10K5 and my sister was 10K6, and that's what the teachers and the other children called us..."

For a number of children this harshness became cruelty. Much of this came from the Mother, less so from the Father, but it sometimes involved acts by other residents:

"We used to see this little boy on The Drive, every night he wet his bed and he was forced to walk up and down with the wet sheet on his head. There was also a girl that jumped or fell out of one of the bedroom windows in Cottage Number 9. She died but no one talked about it so I don't really know what happened..." ***(Girl, resident 1923-37)***

Another girl suffered similarly as far as wetting was concerned as well as bullying from other residents:

"...One of the bigger girls used to get us naked and make us hang from the rafters in the dormitories and I remember getting back into bed, freezing cold. We weren't allowed to leave the room to have a wee, so I wet the bed. Anyone that wet the bed was made to stand naked in the freezing outhouse, for the whole night, with only their wet bedsheet covering them. Because I cried in that cold, my house mother sent me to a psychiatrist..." ***(Girl, resident 1944-51 & 1953-55)***

One boy (resident 1937-45) committed two major offences. First, he and another boy ran away and got as far as Skegness, having taken a bike and been helped by some Land Girls. Eventually they were collected from the police in Spilsby. On their return to Countesthorpe:

"We got twelve strokes with the cane from the headmaster. We had to stand under the clock and he came and gave us two whacks on the hand every quarter of an hour..."

The second time was worse - he took a liking to one of the girls and actually talked to her in her cottage bedroom. Two other boys became involved. Unfortunately another boy informed the House Father:

"...two of the house fathers took all three of us into the school room. They both had sticks and we had to walk round the room and every time we passed them, they beat us with the stick. The girl got sent away and I never saw her again..."

"No one listened to you and they didn't believe you if you said the house mother was bad to you. I was in Cottage 11 and our House Mother was wicked. Many times she'd have us standing in our bare feet on the cold stone floor, hands on heads, way into the night. Sometimes she forgot we were there and left us standing. She beat us with wooden bats and a spoon, although we didn't have the 'flopper', that was only for the boys. Once, some of the girls were being badly knocked about. I was so angry and upset I went to the Residence to tell Matron Adams, but she was ill and couldn't see me, so I left a message with her son. 'It'll be looked into'. But before anything was done, our house mother got to know and she got four of the bigger girls to hold me down and she laid into me with a wooden handle - she went on and on and once she finished she forced me into an ice cold bath. It wasn't until later that I realised that the ice water took away the evidence of the bruises."
(Girl, resident circa late 1930s early 1940s)

Most of the children were cowed by the regime, those that showed rebellion were treated as psychiatric cases and threatened with or actually sent to mental institutions, a practice which continued into the 1950's:

"No one believed you, you had no one to turn to and if you stood up for yourself or spoke out, when you or others were badly treated, you could be sent away, maybe put into a mental hospital - the Towers or the Frith. It nearly happened to me. Me and my friend were working at The Residence and we must have spoken out because we were taken to see the psychiatrist. I remember a long corridor and this man who asked me some things. He had a piece of embroidery I'd done at school and he said 'did you do this?' I said I had and he seemed impressed and said it was good. Maybe they'd said something at school, but any how I didn't get sent anywhere. But the other girl was put in the Frith. I think she was there for years - I don't really know what happened to her..."
(Girl, resident circa late 1930s/early 1940s)

There was a happy ending. She had left the Home unable to read or write to enter service. It was through friends she met in the YMCA (*"No one there ever called me scum"*) that she went to night school.

There is an account of one twelve year old girl actually being sent to a mental institution. She was in the Home in the later 1940's and early 1950's. Apparently the House Mother could not cope with a bright outspoken girl. She was in a mental institution in the south of England for 2 years. Fortunately a member of her family intervened on her behalf. There was eventually a happy ending as she later went into Higher Education and a successful career in business.

Such experiences were clearly at odds with all the rules. The Superintendent and Matron must surely have been aware of some of this as they would be required to sanction punishments and other actions. Many of the cases took place under the jurisdiction of the local authority and not in 'the bad old days' of the Poor Law. In one case cited by a former resident, the Superintendent did dismiss a particularly vicious house father. From some accounts one Matron was not averse to contravening the rules.

Mr and Mrs Harrison who were Superintendent and Matron from 1896 until 1924, displayed a blend of severity and fair-mindedness, yet with compassion and devotion to the children which they reciprocated. Mrs Harrison was described by her daughter-in-law, (daughter of Robert Gee VC, a former boy at the Homes) *"although she was kind, Mother was very formidable and unapproachable"*. She defended the children against the will of the Guardians and instigated a gentler regime with toys at Christmas, prizes for good behaviour and visits to London. Her husband was beloved by the children. Both visited former residents when they went into work to ensure that they were well cared for. Mr Harrison died in 1924 and his wife had to retire and went to live in Wigston and was visited by her 'old girls'. Their successors did not seem to have been so enlightened.

1948: End of an era, dawning of the new!

"Your new National Health Service begins on July 5th.
It will provide you with all the medical, dental and nursing care.
Everyone - rich or poor, man, woman and child - can use it or any part of it.
There are no charges, except for a few special items.
There are no insurance qualifications. But it is not a 'charity'. You are all paying for it, mainly as taxpayers, and it will relieve your money worries in times of illness."
(Official information leaflet)

The old system of health and welfare provision, dating back to the Victorian period, was swept away. In its place the National Health Service had arrived. What was involved? How did it affect people in Leicester?

On the 5th July 1948 they still went to their family doctor. They went to the Leicester Royal Infirmary, City General Hospital and Groby Road Hospital if they were very ill or needed an operation. They still went to Hillcrest if they were too old and/or poor to look after themselves, and the Cottage Homes were still open for orphans. Expectant mothers still went to Bond Street, Westcotes Maternity Home and the City General to have their babies.

The buildings looked the same as the day before - many of them were Victorian edifices. The nurses and doctors looked and behaved in the same way as before - they were still as caring and/or as formidable.

Officially things had changed. You could now enjoy or endure ill health without worrying how to pay because you were a tax payer. If you were too poor, no matter! You had an automatic right to health provision not just for you but for your entire family, and from before birth through to old age and even death. As evidence of this you had your national health card with a number on it - your wartime identity card number. (An administrative convenience!)

The National Health Service was *national*, the same for all people everywhere in the country. The old local hotchpotch of health provision was either swept away or restructured. The most important outcome was that the charity and voluntary organisations were effectively ended - the Victorian legacy was finally removed. The local authorities which had proudly done so much over 50 years to provide health and welfare to the community, saw many of their services transferred to new authorities.

One confusing thing was that everything to do with the hospitals and medical care seemed to come from Sheffield. Medical services were organised on a regional basis - Leicester came under the Sheffield Regional Hospital Board. But why Sheffield? It was understood that each region should have a Medical School. Neither Leicester nor Nottingham had one and Sheffield was the nearest one that had.

Medical provision was divided into three - Hospital and Specialist Services, the Local Authority Service and the General Practitioners Service.

The Leicester Royal Infirmary, along with the Bond Street Maternity Hospital and the Faire Hospital, were taken over by and run by the Sheffield Regional Hospital Board. They were no longer voluntary charities. All the local authority hospitals and related units - The City General Hospital (renamed as the Leicester General Hospital), the City Isolation Hospital and Sanatorium (renamed Leicester Isolation Hospital and Chest Unit), the TB Dispensary (re-named the Chest Centre), Westcotes Maternity Home (renamed Westcotes Maternity Hospital), The Towers Hospital and Glenfrith Hospital and a number of school clinics (Richmond House, Clarendon Park Road and St Albans Road), they all went to Sheffield Regional Hospital Board. At the local level, groups of hospitals and clinics were managed by a series of Hospital Management Committees.

The convalescent homes run by the Saturday Hospital Society were not taken into the National Health Service for reasons never made clear. The Society handed over its ambulance work to the City Council, renamed itself the Leicester and County Convalescent Homes Society, and continued to run two homes.

The role of the family doctor had hardly changed in the previous 50 years. With the introduction of the National Health Service, family doctors still remained independent but worked as salaried contractors to the health service. Their hospital colleagues became paid employees of their hospital. The old panel system was replaced by the local General Practitioners Council. This meant the end of the Leicester Public Medical Service including their dispensaries. Patients could still seek to go to a doctor of their choice, but the General Practitioners Council was responsible for registering patients with a specific doctor. A doctor could refuse to accept you; likewise you could refuse to accept a given doctor. The council had to sort this out and there was some attempt to limit and equalise the doctors' patient lists.

None of this applied to dentists although they also became contractors to the health service. Opticians and pharmacies remained as independent commercial operators although their income came largely from the NHS. You were free to go to any chemist or optician although the latter was not allowed to advertise their business.

The biggest changes were within the local authority sector. Dr MacDonald, Leicester's Medical Officer of Health wrote:

"In its administration of such truly great institutions as the City General Hospital and the City Isolation Hospital and Chest Unit, the Health Committee has every reason to feel very proud. There is no

shadow of doubt that had all the country been equally well served as was Leicester there would have been no need for the Act as far as the Hospital Service is concerned..." ***(MOH 1947)***

The City was left with responsibility for a range of services. Some of them were those they had looked after from the early days of public health, sanitation and food inspection, but other services had been developed over recent years - health visitors, clinics and health education. Under the Act, local authorities were given increased powers and responsibilities which mollified them:

"...On the other hand, the gains, though not as spectacular as the losses are not insignificant. Probably the most important gain is that because the Health Department is no longer required to devote itself to the administration of large hospitals, it can the better put its energy into what really is its proper function, the safeguarding and improvement of the health of the people in its area..." ***(MOH 1947)***

These responsibilities included:

- All local authorities had to set up a Health Committee - Leicester had had one since 1853 although its constitution and membership was revised.
- Provision of health centres - to provide such facilities for general practitioners to develop curative and preventative medicine including maternity, infant clinics, residential and day nurseries and dental care. The City planned to open many more such clinics and facilities.
- Midwifery service - still under the local authority but was now free. The role of the midwife was to be enhanced.
- Home nursing - a completely new service for local authorities. The Health Committee already had close links with the voluntary Leicester District Nursing Association and this was to be extended. The work of health visitors was extended to cover the full age range (Medical Officer of Health saw this as leading to them being social workers).
- Vaccination now voluntary was to be extended from diphtheria to other diseases such as whooping cough.
- The ambulance service - Leicester already had one but it absorbed those run by the Saturday Hospital Society and the St John Ambulance Brigade.
- Preventative welfare services - now a major responsibility to include care, after-care, and rehabilitation.
- Leicester was still responsible for mental care, care of the aged - Hillcrest was now run by the council with the health authority providing the medical care. Child care - the Countesthorpe Cottage Homes and foster homes - remained with the local authority.

So the new dawn came but there were no particular celebrations. For adults with memories of illness and poverty there was considerable satisfaction, also for politicians and others who had fought for a genuine health service for all.

For those in the medical and related professions there were mixed feelings - general practitioners had actually bitterly fought against most of the National Health Act.

Dr MacDonald and his colleagues in public health had regrets at the passing of what they believed to have been a good public health service in Leicester.

Everyone recognised that many of the changes would be difficult to achieve, especially in the post-war economic world. Despite misgivings and regrets and even differences, there was a shared view that the old evils and deprivations of the past had been finally banished and that a new era had dawned, in which health and health care was a right to be enjoyed by all, regardless of age, social class or income.

Postscript 1998

Most of this book was written during 1998 - the fiftieth anniversary of the National Health Service.

Huge advances have taken place in medical science and practice - antibiotics, vaccination and immunisation, X-rays, scanners, laser treatment, replacement of organs, chemotherapy and so on. We have long since eradicated in this country most of the older diseases which afflicted so many people in the past - measles, scarlet fever, smallpox and diseases related to infant and maternal mortality. Their successors - cancer and heart diseases - are now understood and can be cured or contained. TB has been conquered but not quite vanquished. There are some diseases which still perplex us - polio, meningitis and rheumatism for example. There is a generation of 'new' diseases - or were they there all the time? - Alzheimer's, Parkinson's Disease, Legionnaires, M.E., M.S. and Aids, etc.

We now have fewer but bigger hospitals, which have the technical and medical resources of staff and equipment to meet most eventualities. Your stay in hospital has become shorter and you return home and get back to work quickly. The practice of medicine has become essentially a highly technical process.

In Leicester, Groby Road Hospital, Bond Street Maternity Hospital, Westcotes Maternity Hospital, Fielding Johnson Hospital and the convalescent homes have all gone. In their places the Leicester General Hospital and Leicester Royal Infirmary have both become massive complexes, although their remaining Victorian buildings remind us of the past. A new large hospital has since been built - Glenfield General.

'Care in the community' has become part of the healthcare vocabulary. Hillcrest Hospital and the Countesthorpe Cottage Homes have gone and the Towers Hospital has a much reduced role. The residents of all these and other such institutions were dispersed into various forms of sheltered accommodation and now into the wider community, often to their family homes.

The trend towards greater size is seen at the doctor's surgery, with most practices consisting of a team of doctors linked with nurse and health visitor clinics.

People's expectations were raised from the outset of the National Health Service, in keeping with the fervour for change at the time. Such expectations have remained high and we still regard free access to health care as a right. These have been reinforced by the wondrous advances in medicine, engendering a feeling that illness and disease can be overcome.

However, this is at a high financial cost. The 'free' health service has been eroded - there are charges for medicines, spectacles and dental care. We now have an *'internal market'* approach to regulate the use and flow of scarce resources which is supposed to give greater flexibility. Some would say that this has meant the end of automatic access to health care and to the rationing of services.

Local authorities and health authorities faced with tight budgets have cut services, especially homes and facilities for the old and disabled of all kinds. Some would argue that *'care in the community'* is a misnomer for budget cuts.

One response to these developments has been the re-emergence of private medical care, with increasing numbers of people paying into private health schemes. This has led to the building of private hospitals - the most prominent in Leicester being the Nuffield and BUPA hospitals. The greatest development has been the burgeoning growth of private residential care homes for the elderly and others. Some would see this as a return to the socially divisive health system where those with money have access to medical care.

Fears have emerged which stem from a deep disquiet, even disillusionment with our modern health system. Despite the technological brilliance of medical science, be it in the hospital or at the doctor's surgery, many believe that the patient has become the recipient of a series of impersonal procedures directed at the specific ailment. Some people say that we have lost the essential relationship between carer and patient and especially the concern for the wider and deeper emotional needs of the patient.

There is an increased questioning of the *'already-arrived-long-term-effects'* of some of these medical advances - notably the wider use of certain drugs. This is epitomised in the debate over the excessive and often inappropriate prescription of antibiotics and the concern about the effects of them on immune systems - where 'bad' bacteria are becoming resistant yet the 'good' ones are being destroyed.

It is suggested that one consequence of the first concern has been a revival of charitable hospitals, especially hospices where the bond between carer and patient is paramount. Thus we have the Leicester Organisation for the Relief of Suffering (LOROS) next to the former Groby Road Hospital site, and the Rainbows Children's Hospice in Loughborough.

An increasing interest in 'alternative' medicine is seen as a response to both concerns. Alternatives include some of the older traditional therapies but also ones 'imported' from around the world - homeopathy, possibly the oldest, chiropractice/osteopathy, acupuncture, reflexology, aromatherapy, herbalism and others. Such services are now widely available and an increasing number of specialist shops have opened, being joined by 'traditional' chemists. You can even join evening courses to learn about some of them.

Have the hopes and dreams of 1948 been realised? Or are the dreams tarnished or dying?

Appendices

Appendix A Infant mortality rates in Leicester, 1900 - 1950

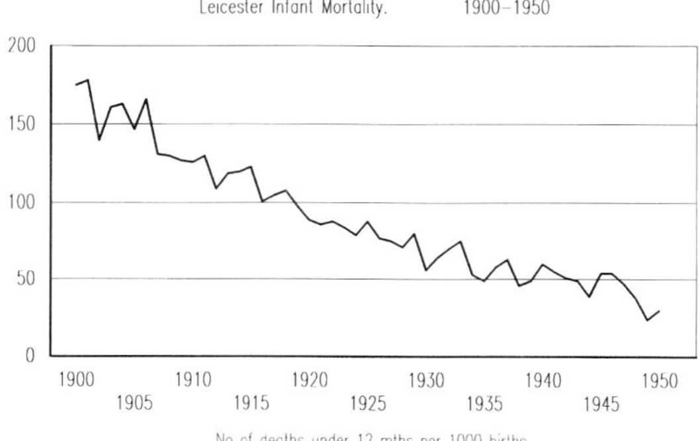

Appendix B Birth and deaths rates in Leicester, 1900 - 1950

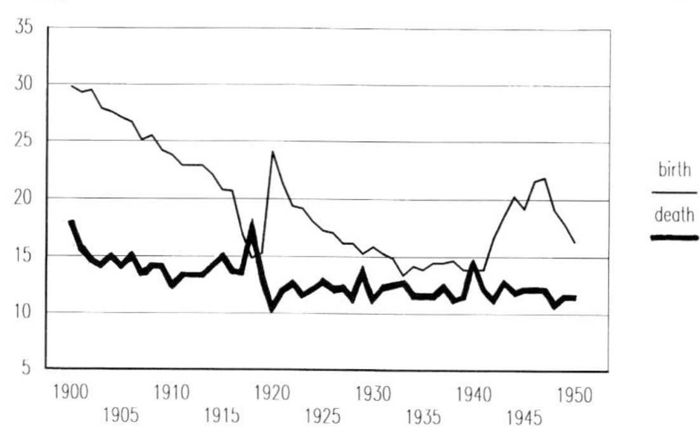

Appendix C Growth of population in Leicester, 1900 - 1950

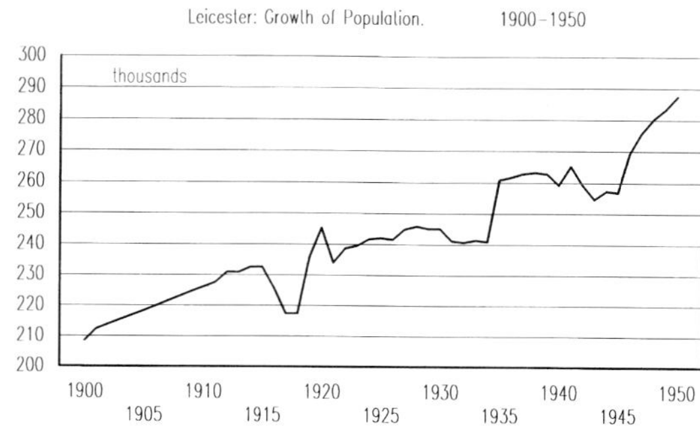

Appendix D Birth and death rates by ward, 1924

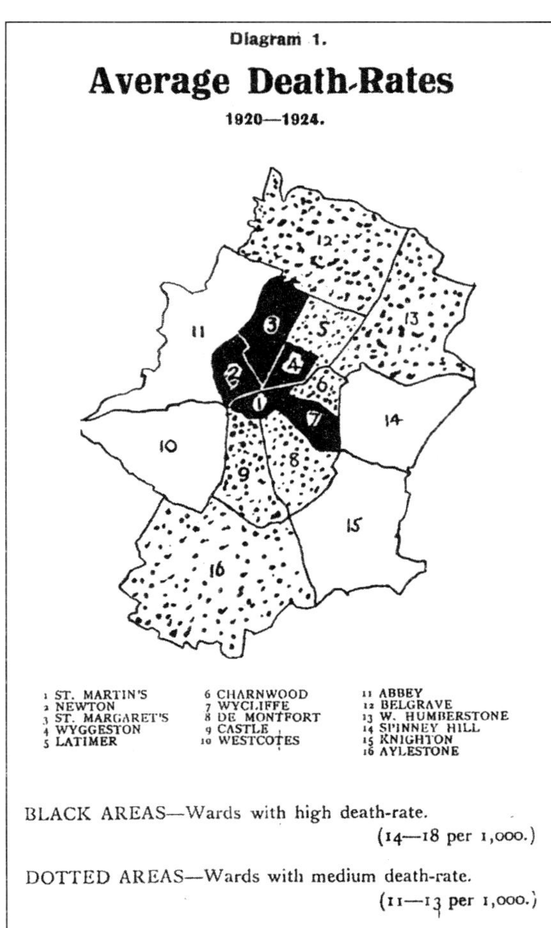

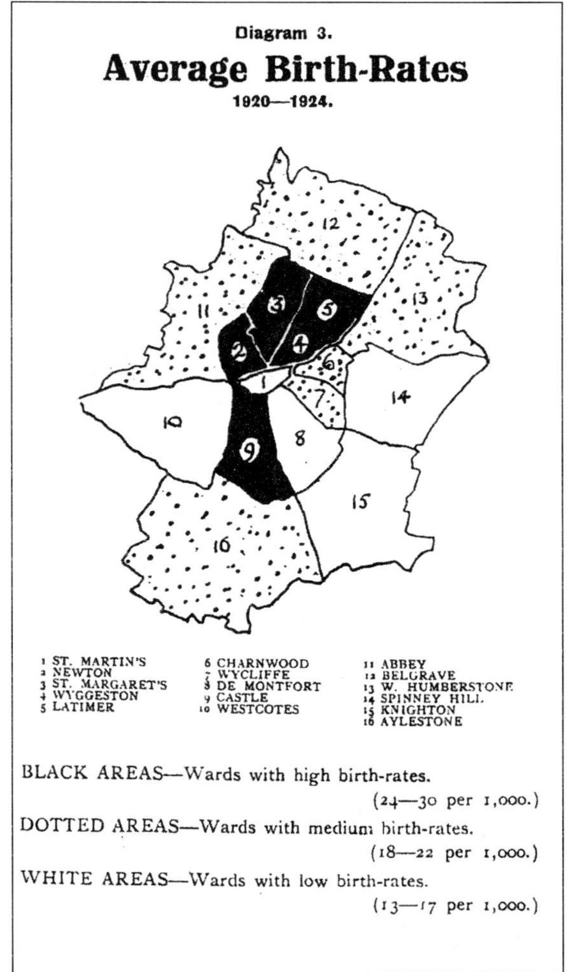

Appendix E How and where the 1903 smallpox epidemic started

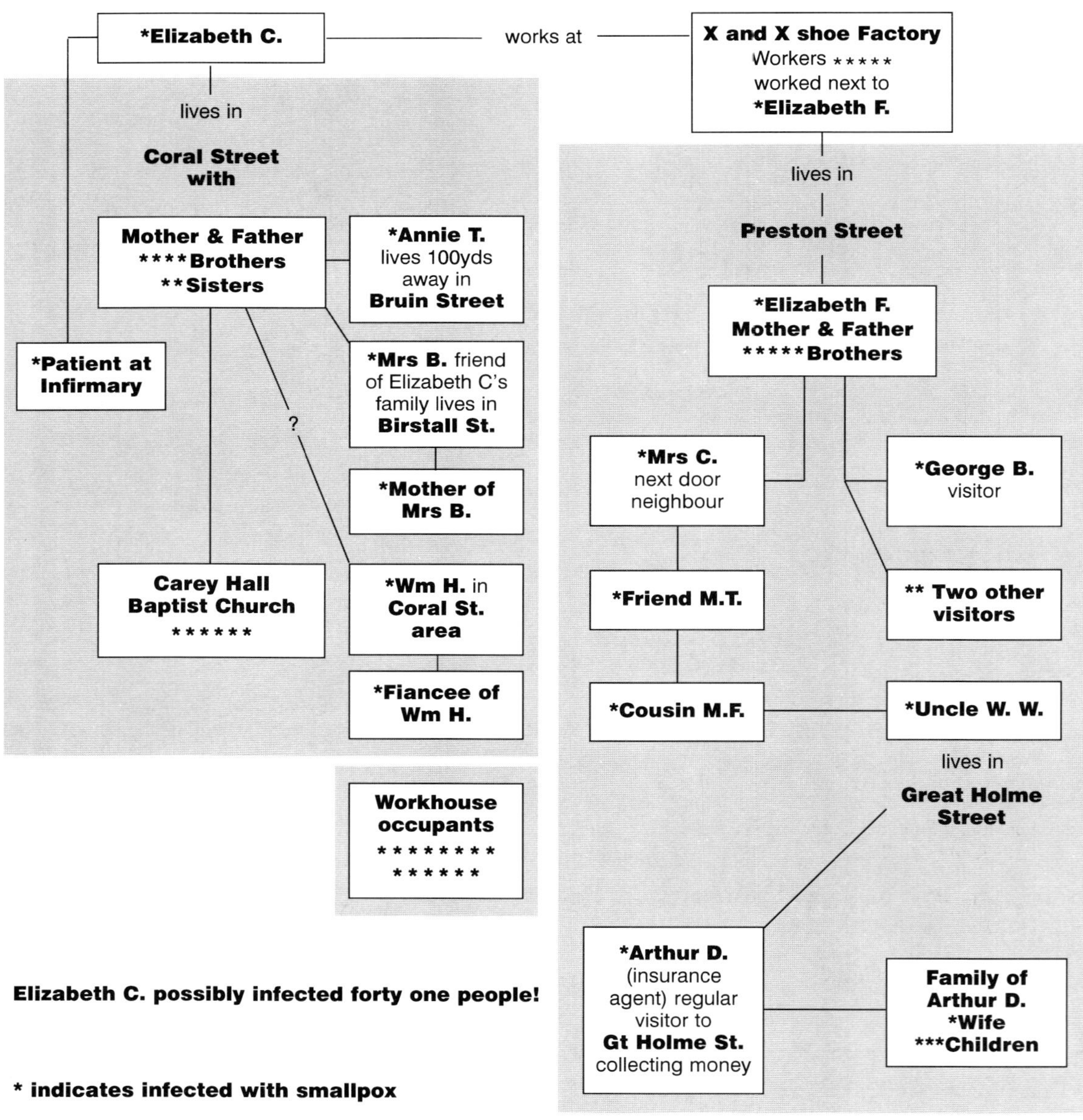

Appendix F Health provision in Leicester 1900-1950

Key to status: C - charity; V - voluntary; P - private; LC - Leicester Corporation; PL - Poor Law Guardians

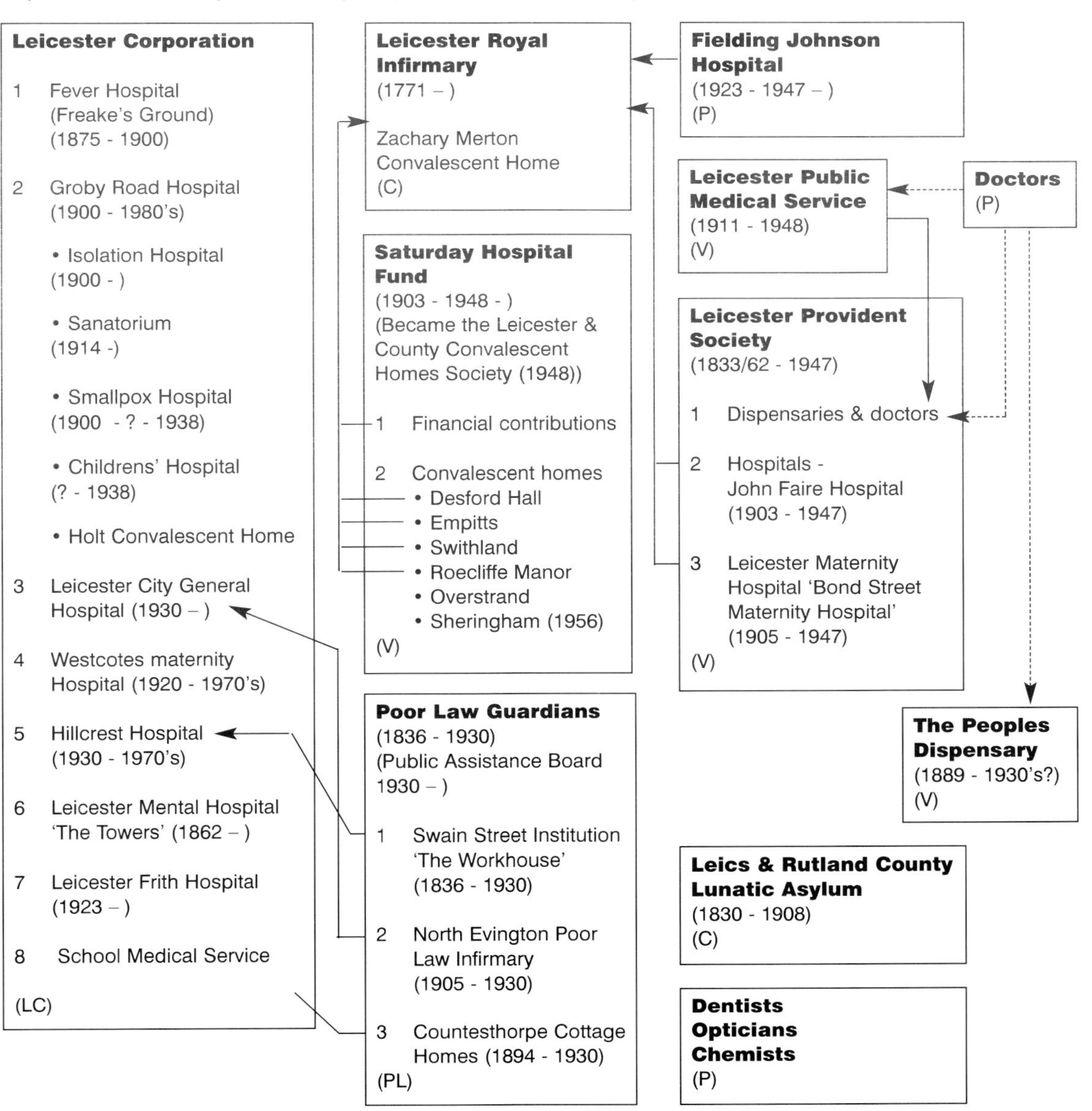

Sources and Reading

Primary sources and newspapers

Borough of Leicester Health Reports; Borough of Leicester School Health Service Committee minutes; Poor Law Guardians/Public Assistance Committee reports, regulations, notices and scrapbook; Leicester Saturday Hospital Society/Leicester and County Convalescent Society annual reports, scrapbooks and Jubilee booklet; Leicester Provident Dispensary/Leicester Public Medical Service rules and regulations; Leicester Children's Holiday Home, 80th year commemoration booklet, annual report; Nurses League Newsletter (Leicester City General Hospital); Kelly's and Wright's Directories for Leicestershire and Rutland; Census of Population, reports for Leicestershire; Prescription Books of W.H. Dennis; Newspapers - Leicester Advertiser, Leicester Evening Mail, Leicester Herald, Leicester Mercury.

Most of these are available at the Leicestershire Record Office.

Books and pamphlets

Aucott, Shirley, *Mothercraft and Maternity* (1997)
Brown, Cynthia, *Wharf Street Revisited* (1995)
Elliott, Malcolm, *Victorian Leicester* (1979)
Frizelle, Ernest & Martin, Janet D., *The Leicester Royal Infirmary, 1771-1971* (1971)
Nash, D. & Reader, D. (eds), *Leicester in the 20th Century* (1993)
Orme, Henry Gilbert & Brock, William H., *Leicestershire's Lunatics* (1987)
Wilshere, Jonathan, *Leicester's Great Influenza Epidemic, 1918-1919* (1986)

Background reading

Howe, G. Melvyn, *Man, Environment and Disease in Britain* (1972)
Kiple, Kenneth F., *Plague, Pox and Pestilence - Disease in History* (1997)
Porter, Roy (ed), *Cambridge Illustrated History of Medicine* (1996)

Other sources

A considerable amount of material in this book was obtained through interviews and discussions.